June 1941
Hitler and Stalin

BOOKS BY JOHN LUKACS

June 1941

Hitler and Stalin

John Lukacs

YALE UNIVERSITY PRESS ◆ NEW HAVEN AND LONDON

Published with assistance from the foundation established in memory of
Amasa Stone Mather of the Class of 1907, Yale College.

Designed by James J. Johnson and set in Carter and Cone Galliard Roman type by
Keystone Typesetting, Inc., Orwigsburg, Pennsylvania.
Printed in the United States of America.

Library of Congress Cataloging-in-Publication Data

Lukacs, John, 1924–
June 1941 : Hitler and Stalin / John Lukacs.
p.   cm.
Includes bibliographical references and index.
ISBN-13: 978-0-300-11437-9 (alk. paper)
ISBN-10: 0-300-11437-0 (alk. paper)

1. World War, 1939–1945 — Campaigns — Russia. 2. World War, 1939–1945 —
Russia. 3. World War, 1939–1945 — Germany. 4. Hitler, Adolf, 1889–1945.
5. Stalin, Joseph, 1879–1953. I. Title.
D764.L817 2006
940.54′217 — dc22
2005057464

A catalogue record for this book is available from the British Library.

The paper in this book meets the guidelines for permanence and durability
of the Committee on Production Guidelines for Book Longevity
of the Council on Library Resources.

10 9 8 7 6 5 4 3 2 1

*This book is dedicated
to Robert Ferrell*

Contents

Contents

Limitations.
Acknowledgments.

This book is less than a monograph but more than a narrative summary. I have been fascinated with German-Russian relations and with Hitler's and Stalin's relations and reactions to each other, especially in 1939–1941, and wrote in some detail about them in my *The Last European War, 1939–1941* (New York, 1976). For that book I had access to German and other archives but not to Russian ones. For this book my limitations include my inability to read Russian, whereby I was also bereft of the at times pleasurable experience of finding and reading all kinds of things in foreign archives. I was, however, able to read many of the Russian documents that have come to the surface during the past twenty years: some of them in their published forms, some of them in German and other translations. A fair amount of the latter I was able to read in the library of the Institut für

Zeitgeschichte in Munich; a goodly amount of Russian documents were translated for me (some orally, some in writing) during and after my visit to Moscow by my Hungarian friend and translator Miklós Nagy, not only fluent in Russian but well versed in the conditions and intricacies of contemporary Russian texts.

I am indebted to him, and in Moscow especially to Professor Sergei Slutsch for his advice and wise judgments; in Munich to the former archivist of the Institut für Zeitgeschichte library Hermann Weiss, as well as to Dr. Jürgen Zarusky; to Professor Plamen Makariev in Sofia and to Vadim Staklo and his wife, Olga Lebedeva, at Yale University Press.

I ask my scholarly and other readers to be indulgent of my admittedly idiosyncratic and consciously imprecise use of "Russia" and "Russian" where "Soviet Union" and "Soviet" would be more accurate; also for Molotov as "foreign minister" and Stalin as "prime minister" when, at the time, commissar for foreign affairs and chairman of the Council of People's Commissars were their titles. I have done this for the sake of descriptive simplicity, at the cost of categorical precision.

2004–2005

June 1941
Hitler and Stalin

CHAPTER ONE

A Historical Perspective

In 1941 the twenty-second of June fell on a Sunday. Before dawn — it was already half-light on this, the longest day of the year — Hitler's German armies invaded the Russian empire, Stalin's Soviet Union. On the evening of the twenty-third of June in 1812, one hundred and twenty-nine years before, French patrols had crossed the Niemen River into Russia, advance guards of Napoleon's Grande Armée that began moving across the next day. Eventually Russia and the Russians defeated both Napoleon and Hitler. But the consequences of their comeuppance were not the same. The Russian triumph over Napoleon confirmed and extended Russia's status as a great European power — a condition that had existed before 1812 and that then prevailed for another century, until 1917. Stalin's triumph over Hitler made Russia one of the two superpowers of the world, and the ruler of eastern Europe—but that condition, the main cause of the so-called "cold war," lasted for less than a half-century, until 1989.

There was a fateful condition of the Second World War that not enough people comprehend even now. This is that the Anglo-American alliance, for all its tremendous material and financial and industrial and manpower superiority, could not have really conquered Hitler's Germany without Russia. That is why 22 June 1941 was the most important turning point of the Second World War. It was more important than Pearl Harbor—because even before Pearl Harbor the United States was already engaged in a virtual naval war with Germany in the Atlantic. It was more important than Stalingrad—because even if the German Sixth Army had conquered Stalingrad, Britain and the United States and Russia would have fought on.

Hitler's war was the last attempt by a European power, and the second attempt by Germany, to rule most of Europe. Napoleon's wars were the last attempts by France to rule most of Europe. Their invasions of Russia led to their downfalls. Consequently the Allies had to share the results of their victories with Russia, both in 1815 and in 1945. But there the parallel ends. In 1945 the division of Europe, and Stalin's occupation of eastern Europe, led to a cold war between Russia and the West. After 1815 this did not happen. In 1914, ninety-nine years later, Russia again entered a European war against the prospect of a single power dominating most of the continent. But in 1917 something happened that was different both from 1815 and 1945. Because of its revolutions in 1917, Russia dropped out of the war. Because of America's entry into the First World War, the Western Allies in 1918 could win the war against Germany even without Russia. This should have given them an enormous advantage, which they misread and mishandled. The results were the largely botched peace treaties in 1919 and 1920, from which Hitler would profit and Germany would rise again. Meanwhile the two Russian revolutions in 1917, especially the Bolshevik one, meant that Russia was weakened, not strengthened.* Few people understood that at the time; few people understand it even now.

But now enough of these perspectives (even though they are perspectives and not speculations). In 1941 and exactly on 22 June 1941, everything depended on two men, Hitler and Stalin. This in itself refutes the social-scientific and current opinion according to which history, especially as we advance into the mass age, is ruled by vast economic and material forces and not by individual persons. The Second World War was not only marked but decided by personalities, by the inclinations and decisions of men such as Hitler, Churchill, Stalin, Roosevelt. To regard Hitler and Stalin

---

*There followed a murderous civil war; Russia lost portions of its empire in eastern Europe; there was a partial famine; the country's agricultural and industrial production fell below their prewar rates for nearly two decades.

as dictators is an insufficient explanation of this. Not all dictators are statesmen, and not all dictators are successful war leaders. But there is something stunning and startling about the relationships of these two men, which is why not only the very events leading up to that twenty-second of June in 1941 but the history of that very day itself is extraordinary. It is that it takes two to start a war. And on 22 June 1941 Hitler wanted a war with Russia, no matter what. He did not present demands to Russia, because he suspected that Stalin might agree to them. At the same time Stalin did not want a war with Germany, he did not want to fight Hitler, all of the rising evidence of the coming German invasion notwithstanding; nor did he believe that Hitler would attack him, because he not only could not but wished not to believe that. This had no precedent in the history of Russia, and few others in the history of the world. But it is this that makes the events — not only before but during that fateful day of 22 June 1941 — so extraordinarily dramatic.

PART I

Hitler and Stalin

CHAPTER TWO

Hitler

"I am relieved of my mental agonies . . ."

I

Hitler's decision to invade Russia developed through stages. The decisive stages were his orders on 31 July 1940 and on 18 December 1940 and on 21 June 1941. On 31 July 1940 he ordered a few of his generals to prepare an — eventual — campaign against Russia; on 18 December he ordered the plans for the invasion, Operation Barbarossa; on 21 June 1941 came the definite and irrevocable instant order "Dortmund," the war to begin early next day. We shall follow these stages, which were not inevitable and not entirely foreseeable. Hitler himself arrived at them after considerable speculation.

Most people, including historians who have written about Hitler, take it for granted that his decision to attack and conquer Russia was inevitable, anchored in his mind from the very beginning of his political life. There are of course multiple evidences of this. They belong in three major categories, overlapping though they are. They involve strategy, German national purposes, and ideology. In his earliest speeches, Hitler stated that Kaiser Wilhelm II and his government were wrong in regarding Britain as Germany's main enemy; that Germany's future lay in the east and not in the west; that the main German effort in the First World War should have been directed at Russia.* Then, in *Mein Kampf* (which he dictated in 1924–1925), as well as in his later speeches and dictated writings, Hitler expounded on his national and geopolitical idea or purpose of *Lebensraum:* that the German people needed, and were entitled, to expand eastward, to conquer at least a portion of European Russia to establish German settlements there, befitting a ruling people.† And finally — I write "finally" because the foregoing two elements may have been in his mind even before 1919 —

* He did not say anything about what Britain and France would have done during and after a German conquest of Russia. Did he think that they, especially Britain, would have simply acquiesced in that in 1914 or after?

† He did not say or write anything about the eastward limits of such a Germanic empire, nor about whether he would allow a Poland to exist between Germany and Russia.

the decisive turning point in his mind and of his career, which occurred not as he said (and as many historians still believe) in Vienna but around his thirtieth year, in Munich, there was his hatred and contempt of Communism. That crystallized during what he saw during the brief Communistic rule in Munich in the spring of 1919. The condition that Russia was no longer a Tsarist state but a Communist one, and the self-asserted center of international revolution, made it the object of his expressed hatreds.

Thus: Russophobia, German expansion, and anti-Communism — these, together with his Judaeophobia seem to have been the mainsprings of Hitler's political, social, ideological, and strategic thinking, driving him ahead. All of this is true, but perhaps not true enough. There was the proverbial Irish biddy, who, answering her neighbors' questions whether the gossip about the young widow at the end of the village was true, said: "It is not true but true enough." The historian, I think, ought to consider something like the opposite: that some things may be true but they are not true enough. That Hitler hated Communists and Communism is undeniable. But consider two caveats. In more than a few instances Hitler said that his contempt for Liberals and Social Democrats was greater than for (in his words, misled) Communists of the working class. More important: he found in 1919 and often thereafter how well he could use the fear and hatred of Communism for his own political purposes: anti-Communism was immensely popular in Bavaria, and elsewhere in the world. He knew how to draw good profit from that. We will see some telling instances of it. My argument is that it is not possible to separate his convictions from his comprehension of the popularity of anti-Communism. He recognized the immensely greater attractions of anti-Communism over those of Communism.

This requires some explanation. Many people, both Communists and their opponents, believed (and many still believe) that the struggles of classes are more decisive and profound than the conflicts of nations; that consequently the international and world-revolutionary propagation of Communism came to represent the greatest and the most dangerous challenge to nations and to civilization—especially after 1917, when Communism and Communists achieved power in Russia, and when Moscow became the center and the focus of the propagation of revolutions. Yet this was not what happened. In the 1790s the ideas and the influences of the French Revolution spread across western Europe, in places even without the presence of the French revolutionary armies. After 1917 every one of the neighbor peoples of Russia in eastern Europe rejected Communism and, when invaded, defeated the Red Army attempting to impose it. Elsewhere between 1917 and 1941 (indeed until 1945 except for Outer Mongolia) the Soviet Union remained the only Communist-ruled state in the world. Meanwhile anti-Communism was a popular ingredient in the civic and political beliefs of almost every nation in Europe—indeed, in most places of the world.

Anti-Communism was not restricted to capitalists or the bourgeois. In Italy it helped Mussolini get into power. In Germany it helped Hitler. And Hitler was clever enough to appear as the principal champion of anti-Communism, not only during his ascent to power but after it. In November 1932 he said to President Hindenburg (who would appoint him to be Germany's chancellor a few weeks later): "The Bolshevization of the masses proceeds rapidly." He knew that this was not so; but he also knew that this kind of argument would impress Hindenburg and his conservatives. Eight months later, in a speech justifying Germany's abandoning the League of Nations, he said: "The Red revolt could have spread across Germany like wildfire. . . . For eight months now we have been waging a heroic struggle against the Communist threat to our people." (This at a time when Communists in Germany had been liquidated, their leaders in prison or fleeing into exile.) In June 1934 he declared to three German Catholic bishops: "The defense of Europe against Bolshevism is our task for the next two or three hundred years."

Not only Germans or conservatives believed this. The idea that National Socialist Germany was a bulwark against barbarian and Russian-supported Communism was held by many kinds of people. (It is believed by some people, not only Germans, even now.) For one thing, this was an important element in "Appeasement," in the political inclinations of many of the British Conservatives, of the majority of their members in Parliament who had been elected in 1935. Hitler knew very well how to draw advantages of that. Hence his establishment of an "Anti-Comintern" pact in 1936, including Italy and Japan, three or four years before his actual military alliance with them; hence his active military support of the Franco side in the Spanish Civil War in 1936–1939, more effective than Stalin's support of the anti-Franco side. (The idea that Hitler's Third Reich represented the defense of "the West," of European civilization against Asiatic or Jewish-Bolshevik Communism, of course, revived at the moment of his invasion of Russia in 1941, attempting to appeal to all kinds of people, eventually attracting more than one hundred thousand non-German volunteers to his armies: but by then that was not enough to prevent his defeat.)

In sum: anti-Communism was an important instrument of Hitler's statesmanship. The still almost universally accepted view of Hitler is that of a fanatic ideologue, with demagogic talents, but one who ultimately courted disaster because he allowed his ideology to drive him, beyond and beneath reason, at the expense of normal political and diplomatic and military savvy. This is a simplistic generalization. So far as his military command went, there were many instances when his generals — and they were among the best, if not *the* best, generals in the world at the time — were right and Hitler was wrong; but there were plenty of other instances, too, when he was right and his generals were wrong. And we must, albeit reluctantly, recognize that Hitler had, and demonstrated, not a few statesmanlike abilities. The purpose of such a statement is not to praise him; rather the contrary: he was a man endowed with talents that he often employed for evil purposes. But the subject of this small book is not that of Hitler's virtues and vices. It is his relationship to Russia and to Stalin. And throughout the history of that there are multiple and telling evidences that his considerations of statesmenship — more precisely: his assessment of his and Germany's situation and prospects — were more important than his ideology.*

There was a duality in the German relationship to Russia before Hitler. The German Republic from 1918 to 1933 was determinedly anti-Communist (as were the German people, except for the minority of Communists among them). At the same time some of the most conservative elements of the German regime, foremost among them the German General Staff, chose to maintain confidential and potentially profitable relations with Russia, whether it was Communist or not. Germany and the Soviet Union signed a nonaggression treaty in 1926. More significant, since 1922 there existed a secret agreement between Berlin and Moscow: providing for German staff officers to go clandestinely to Russia to be involved in some of the training of the Red Army; in

---

* His duality was allied to his secretiveness (a characteristic of Hitler, often obscured by his speechifying volubility). To Admiral Raeder he said in 1939 that he possessed three kinds of secrecy: "the first, when we talk between ourselves; the second, I keep for myself; the third, about problems about the future about which I must keep thinking." Lukacs, *Hitler of History*, 47.

exchange, experimental stations and factories were set up where these officers and their Russian counterparts worked at manufacturing prototypes of armored vehicles and airplanes that the Versailles Treaty had forbidden to Germany. These were things that were significant rather than important: but we must recognize their existence — together with the political geography of Europe at that time, including a Poland, situated between Germany and Russia, regarded as a large unpleasant object by both of them.

Hitler knew of these secret arrangements as a matter of course. He also knew the constraints of his power when he became the chancellor. He could not make a sudden and radical break either with the chiefs of the German army or with the traditional (and conservative) personnel of the German foreign ministry. But within two years of his assumption of the chancellorship he thought that he was strong enough to make changes. He also thought that his public image and posture as a champion of anti-Communism called for them. In 1934 he offered and made a German nonaggression pact with Poland.* He put an end to the secret arrangements of cooperation between the German and Russian general staffs, he ordered the removal of the last few German army officers from Russia. The German ambassador to Moscow, Rudolf Nadolny, opposed to this new course of Ger-

---

* After having ascertained that the substance of Poland's alliance with France was weakening, that neither the French nor the Poles would attack Germany before he could demolish the military restraints imposed on Germany by the Versailles Treaty.

man foreign policy, resigned. His successor was another conservative diplomatist from a very old and historic German family, Count Friedrich Werner von der Schulenburg. We shall meet this impressive person in the course of our story again and again.

But the principal theme of our story is not a history of German-Russian diplomatic relations — or is so only inasmuch as that, inevitably, is an element of the larger story of the relationship of Hitler and Stalin. And at this point of following or unraveling that thread there is another, temporary, constraint: in this chapter, dealing with Hitler and "Berlin" I must, by and large, leave a discussion of many of the initiatives and responses of Stalin and "Moscow" to the next one. Here it may be sufficient to state that after 1933 diplomatic and commercial relations between the Third Reich and the Soviet Union continued to exist, albeit greatly reduced. They were, by and large, maintained in a routine manner, even when Hitler was asserting himself as the leading figure of anti-Communism, and when the German press and propaganda were frothing with innumerable expressions of their contempt and hatred for Communism and the Soviet Union. And of course Hitler's own expressions were more than outbursts of ideological fanaticism. His optimal aim was a German domination of most of eastern Europe, even including the possibility of a future war against Russia if need be, which the Western powers, including Britain, would not oppose, at least not actively. At times he thought that he had come close to achieving this. But some time in early 1939 he came to realize that this was not going to happen, or at least not in the way he had hoped it would. Hence his gradually coagulating decision to arrive at some kind of agreement with Stalin.

But before we get to that dramatic turning point of their relations let me draw some attention to two pieces of essential evidence suggesting that, all of his public (or private) anti-Communism notwithstanding even before that 1939 turning point, Hitler's views of Stalin and Russia were more complex than they seemed and still seem. One of them involves his decision to prepare for war, if war must be. The central document is that of his conference with his leading generals on 5 November 1937, the so-called Hossbach conference, its confidential notes taken by a colonel by that name. This document was selected as a central exhibit at the postwar Nuremberg trials, a proof that Hitler and his generals were preparing for an aggressive war. Its authenticity was questioned decades later, yet its substance remains, by and large, the same. And our interest, now, must be directed at what Hitler said or, rather, did not say about Russia — the kind of Sherlock Holmesian evidence of the dog that did not bark. Hitler spoke of the need to prepare for war, if needed, against Czechoslovakia, no matter what Poland or France or Britain might or might not do. But the significant matter of these Hossbach notes is the absence of almost any mention of Russia — of a Russia that had by then an alliance treaty (upon French urgings) with both France and Czechoslovakia. Why Hitler did not mention Russia we cannot tell. What we can tell is that in November 1937 he evidently did not regard Soviet Russia as an imminent danger.

The other significant element is that of Hitler's thinking and expressions before and during the Munich crisis in 1938. He was not bluffing; he was ready to invade Czechoslovakia in October 1938. But Czechoslovakia had a military alliance with France and also with the Soviet Union. About France, Hitler took his chances: he knew that the French depended on the British; and that the British were unwilling to get into another European or world war less than twenty years after the horrible carnages of the first; and that the French without the British would not fight. He was right. Still, the Czechs (and the French) had that alliance with the Soviet Union. Yet throughout the summer of 1938 and during the very weeks of the culmination of the crisis, there is, significantly, little or no evidence that Hitler gave much, if any serious thought to Stalin's coming into a war against him. He must also have been fortified by the military and diplomatic reports from his embassy in Moscow in August and September to the effect that there was little evidence of Stalin's Russia preparing to go to war with Germany. He also saw that whatever evidence there was about Russian military preparations along the western borders of the Soviet Union, these seemed to be directed not toward Czechoslovakia but against Poland.

At the Munich "conference" Russia was ignored, not only by Hitler and Mussolini but by Chamberlain and Daladier, representing Britain and France. But a few months later this would change; and Hitler was about to consider a profitable accommodation with Stalin.

2

The tentatives and signals and suggestions and approaches and negotiations leading up to Hitler's treaty with Stalin in 1939 form one of the most fascinating and instructive chapters in the entire history of diplomacy. I write Hitler's treaty with Stalin (or Stalin's treaty with Hitler), rather than the German-Russian or Nazi-Soviet or Ribbentrop-Molotov Pact, because the essentials of the treaty depended on those two men, Hitler and Stalin.

It is not possible to determine precisely which of the two made the first signal of invitation. A few people noticed that during the customary reception of foreign diplomats on New Year's Day in 1939 Hitler spoke to the Russian ambassador at some length, the significance of which was exaggerated. There was diminution of German support to Ukrainian nationalism. This was but a tiny straw in the wind. Much more important was Hitler's timetable regarding Poland. That involved not merely Danzig or the so-called Polish Corridor* but the actual independence of Poland. He wanted Polish foreign policy to be entirely subordinated to his wishes. By

---

* Entirely contrary to the British historian A. J. P. Taylor's *The Origins of the Second World War;* see Lukacs *Hitler of History,* 162.

the end of February 1939 he realized that this would not come about. Consequently he began to contemplate the factor of Russia, Poland's big and dangerous enemy, at her rear. (His subservient minion of a foreign minister, Joachim von Ribbentrop, disliked the British and mumbled about the necessity of considering Russia after an indifferent visit to Warsaw.)

A month later, after his march into Prague, Hitler was faced with the suddenly apparent wish of the British and the French — of their governments but, even more, of their public opinion — to arrive at an alliance with the Soviet Union, threatened by Germany as they themselves were; for a grand alliance encircling the Third Reich and thus forcing Hitler to relent from the dreadful prospect of a second world war. But Hitler not only hoped but thought that such a British-French-Russian alliance would not come about; and there were reasons for such a hope. In April the first statements from the Soviet ambassador to Germany suggested that, in Moscow's view, an improvement of German-Russian relations was desirable. Such Russian expressions and signals began to accumulate during the following weeks. On 3 May, Stalin dismissed Maxim Litvinov, his Jewish foreign commissar and a supporter of an eventual Russian alliance with France and Britain; in his stead came Vyacheslav Molotov, then one of Stalin's closest confidants.

Hitler knew what that meant. But he was also cautious. There now developed a triangular tug of war of subtle (or not so subtle) blackmail involving Berlin and London and

Moscow. The British and the French were trying to bring Russia into their alliance system; but they also hoped that this would make Hitler more reasonable. They did not, or could not really believe — nor did the Poles — that Hitler and Stalin could make an agreement between themselves. To the contrary: Hitler allowed a few people to drop hints to the French that contacts between Berlin and Moscow existed and were increasing. By early August — more and more certain that a Western alliance with Russia would not happen — Hitler dropped his caution. He felt pressed for time as his military plans for the war against Poland were approaching; he now wanted an agreement with Stalin as soon as was possible. On 20 August he wrote and sent a personal message directly to Stalin.

Two days later his foreign minister was flying to Moscow. Ribbentrop was anxious about the reception he would receive upon his arrival in the capital of world Communism. He need not have fretted himself. He got a splendid reception. And then Stalin was genial, cordial, happy; they toasted each other; Stalin toasted Hitler. They signed a nonaggression pact. More important: they signed a secret protocol, dividing Poland and northeastern Europe between themselves. Hitler had instructed Ribbentrop to express (though necessarily not in writing) his willingness to extend their agreement even to southeastern Europe if need be, save for German economic interests there.

The news of the pact — it almost goes without saying — was a bombshell, perhaps the biggest bombshell in the modern history of relations between states. It was a great shock for millions of Communists abroad, who had believed in the Soviet Union as *the* main adversary of Hitler. Yet there were relatively few Communists, certainly very few in Russia, who abandoned their loyalty to the Party and to the chimera of International Communism in 1939. Perhaps more significant was the reaction of those millions of anti-Communists and conservatives, both within and without Germany, who had admired Hitler as the champion of anti-Communism. There were hardly any defections from the National Socialist Party. Indeed, the news of the pact first stunned and then exhilarated millions of Germans who saw in this event yet another proof of the genius of Hitler's statesmanship. Power, and its evidences, mattered more than ideology. Most Nazis understood this better than most Communists — while Hitler understood this as well as did Stalin.

In 1917 it was the German General Staff that, at least indirectly, promoted the Bolshevik revolution by arranging Lenin's return to Russia from his exile in Zurich. In 1939 it was Hitler who promoted the reappearance of Soviet imperial power in eastern Europe. (So much for those who claim that Germany was the main bulwark of Europe against Russia and Bolshevism; or that it was Churchill and Roosevelt who handed eastern Europe to Stalin on a platter.) "I put everything on this card," Hitler told Albert Speer on 22 August. Well, not everything: he hoped that his triumph, his agreement with Stalin, would deter the British from going to war with him; he also tried to drive a wedge between the

British and the Poles. Well—in that he did not succeed. However reluctantly, the British and the French declared war against Germany on 3 September 1939. Hitler hoped and thought that in the last minute they would abandon Poland and not choose war; in this he was wrong. But he also thought that they would not enter the war against Germany with full force; in that he was right. In any event—he now had another partner, Stalin.

3

Hitler chose to make this deal with Stalin because of the war coming nearer. But: was this a temporary expedient? Was this but a necessary postponement of his eventual invasion of the Soviet Union? He wanted to give such an impression to certain quarters in the West even before the pact.* His ally

---

*There is a document—an alleged statement by Hitler—that some historians have cited often. Hitler spoke to the Swiss Carl J. Burckhardt, high commissioner in Danzig, a conservative amateur statesman, on 11 August 1939. "Everything I undertake is directed against Russia; if the West is too stupid and too blind to understand this, I shall be forced to seek an understanding with the Russians, defeat the West, and after its defeat turn with all of my forces against the Soviet Union. I need the Ukraine, so that they cannot starve us out, as during the last war." A leading German historian of World War II, Andreas Hillgruber, called this "farsighted," "prophetic." Not so. There are questions (1) about the purpose (2) about the authenticity of Hitler's phrases. Hitler knew Burckhardt's reputation in Paris and London. *If* these were his actual words, they were, rather obviously, meant to be directed to Paris and London *via*

Mussolini and his friends in the Spanish and Japanese governments were temporarily disappointed, but that did not last. Very soon after the pact he would profit from it. Seventeen days after Hitler's invasion of Poland, Stalin's armies entered eastern Poland, advancing to the German-Russian division line agreed upon. As the advancing German and Russian troops met, there were no incidents, only friendliness. Another ten days later Ribbentrop returned to Moscow, for certain adjustments to the secret protocol, exchanging certain territories. Meanwhile, negotiations began for an enormous extension of Soviet-German trade, involving the shipment of masses of raw materials for the Third Reich (which the Soviet Union fulfilled till the very end). The Communist parties throughout Europe were either in disarray or lapsed into inactivity. Hitler realized that his main, and most principled, opponents came from the Right rather than from the Left: monarchists, certain Catholics, and conservatives within Germany and Austria; beyond Germany they were to be Winston Churchill and Charles de Gaulle in the crucial year 1940.

There is another possible indication that, at least for some time, Hitler did not regard his pact with Stalin to be

---

Burckhardt. More serious are the evidences shown by the Swiss historian and biographer Paul Stauffer about Burckhardt's many misquotations (*Sechs furchtbahre Jahre* [Zurich, 1998] and *Zwischen Hoffmansthal und Hitler, Carl J. Burckhardt* [Zurich, 1991]).

About another, frequently cited but evidently forged, document (Stalin's alleged speech of 19 August 1939), see below, p. 56.

altogether temporary. The pact left hundreds of thousands of German minorities within the new Soviet sphere of interest, in the Baltics and later in Bessarabia. Hitler ordered their entire repatriation to the German Reich, to be accomplished wholly and rapidly. This involved, among other things, the extinction of a German presence in Estonia and Latvia after nearly eight hundred years.*

Besides the eastern half of prewar Poland, Lithuania, Latvia, Estonia, and even Finland had been allotted to the Russian side of the secret partition line. Hitler accepted the swift and minatory posting of Russian bases within the Baltic republics without a murmur. Finland was different. The Finnish government knew that to accede to Russian demands (they were mostly territorial and military) could mean the extinction of Finnish independence. The trouble was that the secret protocol, even though geographically precise, did not accurately define the phrase "sphere of interest."† The Finns

---

* It may be significant that when these lands were conquered by the German army in 1941–1942, Hitler spoke little and ordered nothing about the return of these Germans to their ancestral lands: another indication how *Lebensraum* was not then his main priority.

† Much of the same applies to Yalta and to the beginnings of the cold war. Roosevelt's tacit acceptance of the division of central and eastern Europe with Stalin, and the latter's agreement to the generalizations of "A Declaration of Liberated Europe," said little or nothing about what the conditions of governments within the Soviet sphere of occupation would or could be. Stalin interpreted them in his own way, proceeding from the assumption that what was his was his, and the rest of Europe "theirs." Thereafter the aggressive brutalities of his—at first gradual—imposition of Communist regimes in eastern Europe led to the cold war.

had many close ties to Germany. Hitler was not pleased when Stalin provoked a war with Finland and attacked it crudely in late November 1939, but he gave no public or even private expressions of his displeasure. Indeed, German diplomacy and the German press were directed to show no sympathy for Finland during the winter war that ended with a — not entirely total — Russian victory, despite the shockingly poor performance of the Russian armed forces during it.

The Finnish-Russian war was not yet over when Hitler made a new strategic move. He was aware that the French and the British, under the pretext of assisting Finland, were making preparations to land troops in northern Norway, among other reasons to interdict the shipment of Swedish iron ore to Germany, and perhaps even to engage in armed conflict with Russia. This was a harebrained plan that did not mature; but to forestall a later British plan to establish sea and land control over Norway, Hitler on 1 March ordered his navy and army to prepare the German occupation of Denmark and Norway. They did forestall the British and forced them out of Norway in a swift campaign. On 10 May Hitler's army lunged forward into Holland, Belgium, Luxembourg, France. That very day, by coincidence, Churchill became the prime minister of Britain. He would face nothing but disaster after disaster for weeks, save for the evacuation of a mass of British and French soldiers from Dunkirk, which was no victory either. By mid-June, France was collapsing; Mussolini now entered the war on the side of Hitler, who now ruled Europe, or nearly all of it.

Hitler had every reason to be content with Stalin, whose Molotov congratulated Hitler fulsomely for his splendiferous triumphs. Still — on the day Paris fell Stalin and Molotov moved swiftly and brutally to occupy the three small Baltic republics, in order to incorporate them within the Soviet Union. This went beyond the stationing of Russian bases there. Such was Stalin's interpretation of his "sphere of interest." Eleven days later another brutal ultimatum to Rumania led to the Russian occupation of Bessarabia and of another small slice (northern Bukovina) of Rumania. These things began to irritate Hitler. They were not exactly how he had interpreted Stalin's "sphere of interest." Gradually he began to regard Stalin less as an ally, more as a potential adversary. On 31 July in his mountain retreat headquarters he would tell this to a small group of his generals: prepare plans for a war against Russia, yes, Russia.

And why? Because he wished to conquer European Russia all along? Because he feared that one day Stalin might attack him? Why did he think of a two-front war, a war in the east before subduing Britain in the west? Most people think that this was Hitler's greatest and gravest mistake, springing from his ideological mind, a fatal miscalculation stemming from his hubris, the prime and fatal cause of his eventual downfall. There is some truth in these attributions to his thinking, but not enough. Every historical event — indeed, every human decision or act — has multiple causes, but there is a certain hierarchy among them, one being more important, and more decisive, than another. And we may, indeed we must, see what was Hitler's main preoccupation in the high summer of 1940, on that 31st of July. It was not Russia; it was England. There was method, not madness, in his reasoning. He was uncertain about the prospect of defeating the British from the air. "If results of the air war are not satisfactory, [invasion] preparations will be halted." Then came the crux of the matter. "England's hope is Russia and America. If hope on Russia is eliminated, America is also eliminated.* . . . Russia [is] the factor on which England is mainly betting. Should Russia, however, be smashed, then England's last hope is extinguished. . . . Decision: in the course of this context, Russia must be disposed of. Spring '41. The quicker we smash Russia, the better. Operation makes sense only if we smash the state heavily in one blow. Winning a certain amount of territory only does not suffice. A standstill during the winter hazardous. Therefore better to wait, but decision definite to dispose of Russia."

Better to wait. This was an order to prepare plans, not yet a definite directive. That would still take some months. During those months Hitler hesitated — or, rather, pondered his

* About the United States there were two elements in Hitler's calculation. One: once Russia was eliminated, Japan would become an ever greater power in the Far East, and that would keep the United States anxious and busy there. The other, more reasonable, expectation: after the elimination of the Soviet Union, how could Roosevelt and Churchill expect to defeat the Third Reich in Europe? Would not people in America (and even in Britain) turn against them? With Germany invincible, and with at least Communism eliminated, how much sense would there be to go on waging an unwinnable war against him?

strategy, his chances. But underneath his calculations — or, rather, tying them together — ran the main thread (that main thread that ever so often governs the decisions of all kinds of people): the wish to convince himself that his eventual decision was correct, unquestionable, the right one. His eye now battened on every kind of evidence, including the smallest ones, that Russia was not to be trusted. Yes, there were such evidences: but they amounted to less than the overall condition, which was that Stalin still wanted to trust him, indeed, to be his ally. There was not the slightest sign that Stalin did or even wished to improve his relations with London (or with Washington). Vast and valuable freight trains rumbled across the Polish plains, bringing from Russia to Germany stuff for the German war industry. And there was the German ambassador in Moscow, the spare, upright Schulenburg, whose lucid dispatches to Berlin suggested his conviction that Stalin had no wish to quarrel with Germany.

But there were troubles. There were the first signs of a change in German policy involving Finland. Moscow was putting pressure on Finland again. Berlin (more exactly, Field Marshal Hermann Göring) now offered some support to the Finns. For the first time since the Hitler-Stalin pact, a small German military mission arrived in Finland. Meanwhile Moscow suggested to Rome that a Russian agreement with Italy might lead to another reciprocal-sphere-of-interest deal in the Balkans. Stalin was not pleased with the spread of a German presence in the Balkans, to Rumania first of all; there was a carefully worded Russian protest against that. And, to counterbalance the Germans in Rumania, Russia should have its privileges in Bulgaria, to say the least. Hitler did not want that. At the same time he turned to a larger deck of cards to play. On 16 September he canceled his directive for preparing the invasion of England. A day or so later he proposed a grand three-power alliance to Japan, with Germany and Italy. The Japanese jumped at this chance at once. This Tripartite Treaty included a curious clause, with few or no precedents in the language of diplomacy. It stated that this alliance between these three great powers was *not* directed against the Soviet Union. It was evidently directed against the United States, where Roosevelt was now drawing closer and closer to Churchill.

While the bombing of London went on and while Hitler pondered where the prime direction of his strategy next should be (perhaps in the Mediterranean, against Gibraltar?), he agreed, upon Ribbentrop's insistence, to a — perhaps last — effort to solidify, indeed, to extend, the essence and the scope of German-Russian relations. This would be a routine returning of Ribbentrop's historic mission to Moscow. Now Molotov would come to Berlin.*

Molotov arrived in Berlin on 12 November. What then

---

* Interestingly enough, this was the first time that an American presidential election played a role in the great affairs of the world: Stalin thought it best that Molotov's visit to Berlin should come after the American election in November. On the other side Hitler was critical of Mussolini for having attacked Greece in late October — again, before the American election.

happened was a dialogue of the deaf. The deafer of the deaf was Molotov—mostly because of his personality, which was that of a wooden and unimaginative dolt. Hitler was unimpressed with him, to say the least. Hitler, and especially Ribbentrop, suggested and hinted at large vistas, possibly even including the Soviet Union in a grand Eurasian alliance, together with Italy and Japan. Molotov kept pecking and pecking away at Bulgaria and Finland like a shortsighted woodpecker. Ribbentrop tried to smooth things out but largely in vain.* Largely: because Hitler was both angered and relieved by Molotov's ways. He was angered by the Russian's obstinate pettiness. At the same time he was relieved that his inclinations of not wanting further agreements with Russia were right.† After Molotov returned to Moscow, Stalin smelled trouble. He told Molotov to draft a message to Berlin suggesting that the Soviet Union might join Germany and Italy and Japan in a grand alliance, leading to a potential

---

* When Churchill came to Moscow in August 1942, Stalin told him a story. The British had sent a few planes to fly over Berlin and drop a few bombs during the Molotov visit. According to Stalin, when Molotov and Ribbentrop walked down to the air raid cellar, Ribbentrop urged Molotov to enter into worldwide alliance, whereupon Molotov said: "And what about Britain?" "Britain," said Ribbentrop, "is finished." Molotov: "If Britain is finished, why are we going down to the cellar and whose are the bombs that are dropping?" Churchill found this amusing enough to include it in his war memoirs. I am convinced that not one word of it is true.

† Hitler's confidential directive (no. 17) on 12 November: "No matter what the results of these negotiations all previous preparations for the East [Russia] must be continued." Manfred Messerschmitt, in Pietrow-Ennker, *Präventivkrieg?* 27.

division of the world, Russia's share being mostly the Middle East. Ribbentrop's heart may have leaped, but Hitler did not even deign to answer. On 18 December he issued his directive for the invasion of Russia, Operation Barbarossa.*

4

More than six months would pass between the directive and 22 June 1941. Many things would happen during that time. But Hitler's mind did not change. It is interesting that he did not keep his distrust of Russia very secret. Even before the Barbarossa directive Hitler made oblique statements to foreign statesmen on occasion, suggesting that he might be forced to settle his accounts with Russia. He did this not only to influence potential allies for joining an eventual war against the Soviet Union; there are reasons at least to suspect that he wanted London to know something of this. And why? Had he not said and thought that Russia was England's last hope? Yes: but he still thought that there were people in London who would understand that his main aim was to destroy Russia rather than the British Empire. What is not a

* "The German Armed Forces should be prepared *to crush Soviet Russia in a quick campaign* even before the conclusion of the war against England." "I shall order *the concentration* against Soviet Russia possibly eight weeks before the intended beginning of operations." "The ultimate objective of the operation is to establish a defence line against Asiatic Russia from a line running approximately from the Volga River to Archangel . . ."

conjecture is his indifference to keeping the German war preparations against Russia very secret. After March 1941 this would have been impossible in any case: the massing of ever more troops moving up to the German-Russian demarcation line could hardly be hidden.

Meanwhile Stalin had sent a new ambassador to Berlin (who, among other things, carried a personally signed photograph of Stalin with him); this, and other Russian gestures, did not impress Hitler. But there was now friction between Russia and Germany, involving the Balkans. The First World War had broken out in the Balkans; the Second World War did not; in 1914 the Balkans were the powder keg of Europe, but not in 1939. The Hitler-Stalin pact divided the northeastern and central-eastern portion of Europe between themselves, but not the southeast. Then, to Hitler's dismay, in October Mussolini upset matters by attacking Greece. The Greeks proved brave, fighting the Italians off, and Hitler knew that the British would profit from that. He had already attached Hungary and Rumania to his three-power pact; there was now a mass of German troops in the latter country. He would now move into Bulgaria and make first Bulgaria and then Yugoslavia adhere to that pact and to the German alliance system. The Russians, for more than one reason, insisted that at least Bulgaria should belong to their sphere. Hitler, already irritated by Molotov's harping on Bulgaria when in Berlin, paid no attention to that. The few Russian diplomatic protests concerning Bulgaria were dismissed as if they did not matter. On 1 March the German army began moving into Bulgaria. There was now a serious cause of conflict between Berlin and Moscow. Yet it did not mature into such. Stalin did not want that to happen. As a matter of fact, a memorandum of the German Foreign Ministry stated that in March, Soviet supplies to Germany "rose by leaps and bounds."*

That memorandum was dated 5 April. On that day arose another conflict between Germany and Russia, now about Yugoslavia. Hitler wanted Yugoslavia to join his Tripartite Pact. The Yugoslav government agreed, reluctantly. But then occurred something like a Serbian national uprising against the government, a coup d'état nudged, abetted, and financed by the British. The new Yugoslav regime hoped to remain "neutral"; but Hitler reacted in an instant, ordering the invasion and the destruction of Yugoslavia. Again he kept nothing secret about that. His powers of insight were significant: he said that while the British abetted the coup in Belgrade,

---

* "At our request, the Soviet government even put a special freight train for rubber at our disposal at the Manchurian border." *Nazi-Soviet Relations, 1939–1941*, 318–319. Hereafter abbreviated *NSR*. Documents from the Archives of the German Foreign Office. Ed. Raymond James Sontag and James Stuart Beddie. Department of State, Washington, D.C., 1948 — at the very beginning of the so-called cold war. (Walter Lippmann wrote that this publication was unduly hurried.) It was made possible because of the American capture of about 90 percent of the archives of the German foreign ministry, the documents of which had been microfilmed. In the following fifteen or more years many of these documents were printed in *Akten zur deutschen auswärtigen Politik 1918–1945*, series D, vols. 10–11. During previous researches I checked the translated documents in *NSR* with the original German texts. They were invariably correct.

people in the Balkans thought that the Russians were behind it. In reality, the Russians had had nothing to do with the coup. But then they thought they ought to make at least one small gesture. After all, they had divided northeastern Europe with the Germans, but in southeastern Europe they had gotten nothing: Rumania, Bulgaria, Albania, and now Yugoslavia, all of them in the German sphere, with Greece coming up. At one o'clock in the morning of 6 April, Stalin in Moscow signed a nonaggression treaty with Yugoslavia. The Yugoslav minister in Moscow, exhilarated, drove back to his residence at dawn,* in the very hour when squadrons of the Luftwaffe rose from German airfields to pound Belgrade into ruins.

That Soviet-Yugoslav treaty was not much more than a gesture: Russia and Yugoslavia were hundreds of miles apart; how would they ever "aggress" against each other? Most gestures possess a certain meaning; but if they have no consequences they become meaningless. So it happened, because Hitler's armies overran Yugoslavia in hardly more than a week. Instantly Stalin recognized a new situation and its potential dangers: that was, what would Hitler be thinking? A week after his now meaningless gesture-treaty with the Yugoslavs, he made another much more meaningful gesture (to which we shall yet return), now to impress the Germans and Hitler, to assure them of his solid friendship.

* The Russians carefully predated the treaty to 5 April.

This, too, meant nothing to Hitler. He was determined to crash into the Soviet empire and crush it. He had already ordered instructions of various kinds, admonishing officials and the army that this coming war with Russia would be different from other wars, not subject even to the few international limitations of warfare between states.*

There was, however, another matter in Hitler's mind that was involved with his plans against Russia. It involved America via Japan. "England's last hope is Russia and America": he returned to this argument again and again, adding that Russia was the principal thing, because against America he could do nothing—except for this: "If Russia is eliminated," Japan would become an ever greater power, causing plenty of worry for the United States. Well, in September 1940 the Japanese joined Hitler's global alliance pact. Yet this did not deter Roosevelt from allying himself closer and closer to the British. Now the Japanese had a dilemma. They had already occupied large portions of China and, after the French collapse, established themselves in French Indo-China. Should they plan to profit more from a European

*The key document is Hitler's speech on 30 March to more than two hundred generals, lasting more than two hours: "A war of annihilation." "The Russian soldier is no 'Kamerad.'" "A war between two views of the world." "Bolshevism amounts to criminality." *And yet here, too, the duality of his purposes:* "England at this time puts its entire hopes on Russia and America." Below, *Als Hitler Adjutant,* 266. Again on 14 June: "If we lose this war then all Europe becomes Bolshevist. If the English do not see and understand this . . ."

war, as they indeed had in 1914–1918? Their highest circles were divided. They sent their Foreign Minister Yōsuke Matsuoka to visit Berlin, via Moscow, by rail.

Matsuoka, once a student in the United States, was a despicable man. In Berlin he kept grinning and grinning at Ribbentrop, making bad jokes about the English (his Japanese attempts at wit even worse than Ribbentrop's north-German absence of humor). Ribbentrop told Matsuoka "confidentially" that "present relations with Russia were correct, to be sure, but not very friendly." Then Hitler told Ribbentrop and Matsuoka to come over to him, at once. He gave a long monologue about the world situation. England had already lost the war. America was England's last hope, but there Japan could help. If, for example, the Japanese took Singapore, Roosevelt could not do much. "The second hope of England was Russia." (An interesting reversal of what he had said a year before: that Russia was the first, not the second, of Churchill's hopes.) Matsuoka's response was worse than slippery; it was slimy: his words were those of a traitor to his own government. Of course he agreed with the Führer about everything. It was only that the high court and certain politicians in Japan were hesitant to act "partly from a pro-British or pro-American attitude." He told Hitler that on the way to Berlin he had stopped in Moscow. Now he had to tell the Führer something in confidence. He wanted to make not more than a short stop, but Stalin wished to see him. He had told Stalin that the Japanese were not capitalists but "mental communists" and that "the Anglo-Saxons were the common foe of Japan, Germany, and Soviet Russia." Stalin agreed and said that he wanted to see Matsuoka again on his way back from Berlin; he also said that "Soviet Russia had never gotten along with Great Britain and never would." Matsuoka had two more talks with Ribbentrop and one more with Hitler (he had gone to Rome to see Mussolini and the pope in the meantime). Ribbentrop said that it was at least "possible that Russia would set out on the wrong road, although he did not really expect that from Stalin. But one could not know." Matsuoka "then asked whether the Führer considered the possibility of a Russian-Japanese-German alliance." Ribbentrop said no: "If Germany should feel herself endangered, she would immediately attack and put an end to Bolshevism." When Matsuoka saw Hitler for the last time, Hitler said little about Russia: "The enemy no. 1 was America." Matsuoka said that the trouble was the existence of high circles in Japan who did not share his views.*

So much for the character of this foreign minister and supposed diplomat, representing his own country and its rulers abroad. On his way back to Tokyo, Matsuoka again stopped in Moscow, longer than expected. Stalin asked him to the Kremlin. He proposed a nonaggression treaty with Japan, which Matsuoka instantly accepted. There followed an unusual midday banquet, with much drinking by everyone.

The consequences of this Russian-Japanese pact were

---

* *NSR,* 280 et passim.

great, both in the short and in the long run. Its immediate consequence was an extraordinary scene at the Moscow railroad station (about which see the next chapter). The long-range consequence was that Japan did not go to war with Russia in 1941 — something that Hitler did not mind, until much later. Near the end of his life Hitler ruminated about why he had to go to war with Russia and regretted that he had to go to war with America. By then it was very, very late.

5

The unexpected German war in Yugoslavia and Greece delayed Barbarossa by about five weeks. The massing of an enormous German army pressing against the long land frontiers of the Soviet Union took time. Besides, this was something that could not remain secret. We have seen that Hitler had no intention to keep it very secret either. But now, rather suddenly, he had an alternative that he had not considered. His army did not only scatter the Yugoslav army; other German divisions, issuing from Bulgaria, overran Greece in another fortnight and forced the British there to undertake another, rather ignominious, evacuation. After that Hitler agreed to a daring plan, the conquest of Crete with airborne troops. The battle was close but the Germans won. Even before the end of May the way for a German invasion of the Near or Middle East seemed open. There was a revolt in Iraq against the British; the Vichy government in France was not about to deny the Germans landing rights in Syria and Lebanon, then still under French colonial rule. Meanwhile General Erwin Rommel had beaten the British back to the western frontiers of Egypt. Had Hitler willed it, German troops could perhaps have arrived at the gates of India emulating Alexander the Great. Hitler did not choose to do so (unlike Napoleon who could not do so in 1799 because of the British).

His priority was Russia. Mussolini and the Japanese were not altogether happy with that, but they could hardly object. The same goes for some of the high officials of the Third Reich. They said little and did nothing. There was one exception: Rudolf Hess. He was nothing less than Hitler's designated deputy Führer (and also titular leader of the National Socialist Party), Hitler's close friend and follower for two decades. He believed in Hitler's words in *Mein Kampf* even more than did Hitler. For Germany war with Britain was a tragedy; the destiny of Germany was in the east of the continent. Hess had seen little of Hitler since the war began. He, too, had a group of advisers and friends (including a geopolitician and an astrologer). He now grasped a thin thread of destiny in his own hands. He flew off to Britain. His flight was unique, daring, sensational, precise. His expectations were not. He dropped out of a black sky on the night of 11 May, near the house of the Duke of Hamilton. Hess had had a pleasant encounter with the duke a few years before during the Olympic Games in Berlin. Hess thought that the duke was very close to King George VI; that he could thereby impress what he thought was a British peace party. The condition sine qua non was that Churchill had to go. To his interviewers Hess said that Hitler abhorred waging war on the British people. He did not say anything about a coming German war on Russia.

This was a fantastic occurrence; but it had almost no effect on the course of events. Hess interpreted Hitler's wishes rightly; but his adventure was senseless. Hess did not fly off in accord with Hitler. The latter, single-minded, was furious. Stalin, hardly less single-minded, thought that the entire Hess affair could mean a collusion between Britain and Germany at his expense. Churchill was pleased, though not as much as Hitler thought he would be. Hitler and Josef Goebbels were surprised that the British did not make more propaganda of the Hess episode.* Then there came a more important plus for British morale. The massive German air assaults on Britain were diminishing. Most of the German air force was now moved east, deployed for the coming Russian war. Churchill was now certain that Hitler had decided to move eastward. Stalin was not. Hundreds of items of information about the amassing of German divisions in Poland were funneled to Moscow from dozens of sources; but

---

*There may have been one reason for that. Unlike during the first months of the Blitz, British morale was not high in May 1941, partly because of the successive British defeats in the eastern Mediterranean, partly because of the severe bombing of British cities, especially London (which had suffered the heaviest German attack on the night before the Hess flight).

Stalin was not inclined to believe them; he believed that the British were trying to cause trouble between himself and Hitler. So from early May on, he made one move after another, one gesture after another to impress Hitler with an unalterable Russian decision for friendship with Germany. These were not minor matters; but they had no effect on Hitler. More than a week before 22 June he began to advise his potential allies (Rumania and Finland, and even the Hungarian general staff) to prepare for a war against Russia. In the early afternoon of 21 June he dictated a long letter to Mussolini. "Duce! I am writing this letter to you at a moment when months of anxious deliberation and continuous nerve wracking are ending in the hardest decision of my life. . . . Since I struggled through this decision, I again feel spiritually free. This partnership with the Soviet Union, in spite of the complete sincerity of the efforts to bring about a final conciliation, was nevertheless often irksome to me, for in some way or other it seemed to me to be a break with my whole origin, my concepts and my former obligations. I am happy now to be relieved of these mental agonies."*

The order for "Dortmund," to start the invasion, went out at 7 P.M. Berlin time, on 21 June, a Saturday evening.

---

* *NSR*, 352–353.

CHAPTER THREE

Stalin

"He would not begin the war . . ."

I

That Stalin did not want war in June 1941 — that much we know. But: did he want war at another time, a war of his own choosing? Did he not expect, and hope, that the other European powers would exhaust themselves in a great war, after which the Communist Soviet Union, unbroken and powerful, would enter Europe and dominate it?

Yes and no. Yes: that was a Communist expectation: after a great war between the capitalist powers they, no matter who the relative victor, would barely survive, badly mangled and torn, at a time when Europe would be ripe for the advance of Communism athwart the continent. No: Russia must be ready for a great war but not seek it: expand where and whenever possible but not at the risk of war with a great power; rather in agreements forced out from the latter.* And those were expectations not of a Communist but of a statesman. And by 1939 Stalin had become a statesman, because developments in the world well nigh forced him to be one; but then this corresponded, by and large, with the development of his personal inclinations. He had begun seeing himself as a statesman; first and foremost a statesman; above all other considerations, a statesman. So to his development as a statesman we must now turn.

Now, more than fifty years after his death, and more than fifteen years after the demise of the Soviet Union and of much of its empire, there exist more than one hundred biographies and books about Stalin — fewer than biographies and books about Hitler, which is understandable. Hitler: he was a great exception, rising from near-nothing, the sole maker of the Second World War, a planetary genius who had no precedent in the history of Germany. Stalin: his rise to power was impressive, too: but he did, in many ways, fit into the thousand-year-old history of his unhappy people, in some ways reminiscent of Ivan IV, named the Terrible.† Be-

---

* Andrei Zhdanov on 20 November 1940: "Ours is a unique kind of neutrality — we gain certain territories without going to war." Slutsch, in Pietrow-Ennker, *Präventivkrieg?* 95.

† "Ivan Grozny" in Russian, where the adjective *grozny* also means

cause of this, all of the recent and fashionable intellectual comparisons of Hitler and Stalin miss the mark, indeed are senseless: who was the greater murderer of the two? "Numbers," as Kierkegaard once said, "are negations of truth." Hitler was an Austrian who saw himself as a German, destined and capable to lead the German people at a given time; Stalin was a Caucasian Georgian who wanted to lead the peoples of the Soviet Union, perhaps foremost among them the Russians: but there the parallel ends. The Germans whom Hitler inherited were the most educated people in the world. The peoples whom Stalin came to rule were not. That is why the fanaticism and the brutality and the mass killings ordered by Hitler and committed by Germans were, and have remained, more shocking and unexpected than the brutalities and murders ordered by Stalin and committed by his underlings; and that is, too, why Hitler remains more interesting and more extraordinary than Stalin (and National Socialism than Communism). It is unfortunate (to say the least) that so many writers and historians and biographers of Stalin, including honest ones, fall back at defining him as a representative of extreme Marxism, a fanatic dogmatist who used every means for its cause. This is nonsense or, at best, near-nonsense: Stalin's personality, his brutalities, were not those of a dogmatic Marxist but those of a Caucasian chieftain.

And while this small book is not a biography of Stalin, we

---

something more than "terrible," suggesting the somehow positive or even admiring sense of "awesome."

must say something about his character, inasmuch as that may help us to comprehend something about the great dénouement of the great drama of the twenty-second of June, nineteen forty-one. Suspicion, cunning, secretiveness, rudeness were sinews of his character and instruments of his willpower. Thus he came to power and solidified it. He was not intellectual, though he read much (so did Hitler); he knew little of the outside world (less than Hitler). His enemy Trotsky knew much more of the world beyond Russia and much more about books and much more about Marx, but all of that served him not much: he was — allow me to say this — a fool. Their conflict was the — not unprecedented, not even unusual — one between brain and brawn; between a highly clever man and a powerful suspicious one, each unscrupulous in his own way. What is relevant to our story is the conflict between their views of the outside world, about which Trotsky thought that he knew much and that Stalin didn't. The first believed in the cause and even in the possibility of international revolution, the latter much less so and, perhaps, not at all. Suspicion is an odd condition of the human mind. It may be the outcome of knowing too little or, to the contrary, of knowing too much: it may be the result either of deep-seated ignorance or of willful speculation. Stalin, while largely ignorant of the world outside Russia, also knew the backwardness and weakness of Russia. Hence his 1925 slogan: "Socialism in one country" — which, at that time, was not really a break with the Communist dogma and propagation of international revolution but only a realization of first things first.

None of this should even suggest that he was a man of great or profound wisdom, surely not between 1925 and 1939, from his coming to power to the final and extreme consolidation of his power (that also coincided with the coming of his pact with Hitler). The record of Stalin's rule, from 1928 to 1939, is horrible. It beggars belief. It is that of the collectivization and of the purges, two pale words that mean nothing unless we know what they involved: the evidently uncalled for deaths of millions, a near-famine, and mass executions on a scale unmatched through centuries. Through the 1930s, when Adolf Hitler made Germany the most powerful nation in Europe, with the overwhelming majority of a confident people behind him, under a relentless German sun, the impression of Josef Stalin's Soviet Union — except of course for Communist intellectuals and believers across the world — was that of a dark and sullen mass of a country, suppurating with boils and bleeding from thousands of wounds. But my task and purpose here is not that of comparison. It is to detect symptoms, early symptoms, of the progress of Stalin's mind, leading him from internationalism (never a strong strain in that mind) to nationalism; more precisely, the evolution of Stalin the revolutionary to Stalin the statesman.

Very telling (at least to the eyes of this historian) was his increasing concern with the powers of the state. This is especially significant, because for Marx and Engels and even Lenin the state was the enemy; the real struggles in history were not between states but between classes; the state must be weakened, not strengthened; and at the triumphant end of socialism's march forward, the state, so Marx wrote, "will wither away." In Stalin's mind the opposite was true, and also desirable. There are early evidences of this. In a message to his minion Sergei Ordzhonikidze in September 1931 Stalin criticized the Politburo, and particularly Lazar Kaganovich (the Jewish member of the Politburo). "What is better" Stalin asked and wrote, "putting pressure on the state's reserves of foreign currency while preserving the peace of mind of the economic apparatus, or putting pressure on the economic apparatus while preserving the interests of the state? I think the latter is better than the former." During the 1930s Stalin read book after book about the histories of tsars. In 1935 he said to his close circle: "The people need a Tsar whom they can worship and for whom they can live and work."* There is really no rational explanation of the terror of the purges. They were inseparable from the brutality and suspiciousness of Stalin's Caucasian character (many of his cruelest executioners were also Caucasians): the inclination to eliminate anybody who may not be an actual but a potential critic, let alone opponent; and, for the sake of safety, the more of that kind is liquidated, the better. But there may be a, perhaps partial, explanation of those otherwise senseless purges of the 1930s: the replacement of a party bureaucracy by a state bureaucracy, wholly subservient to Stalin. For our purposes it is important

---

* Montefiore, *Stalin,* 177. Molotov: "Ivan [the Terrible] killed too few boyars. He should have killed them all, to create a strong state." Ibid., 231.

to recognize how by 1939 the word *state* had become sacrosanct in official Soviet terminology, in the Soviet press, and in other publications: "state security," "state power," "state interests" — sanctified, and more reverend even than the interests of the party.

It may be more than a coincidence that Stalin ordered the winding down of the purges around the time when he also ordered a change in the course of the giant Soviet state, the first cautious move of the tiller, setting a tentative turning toward Germany. But before we come to our main subject, that of the relationship between Stalin and Hitler, we must take a glance at Soviet foreign policy before 1939, recognizing something that made (and perhaps still makes) Russian foreign policy, indeed, Russian history, differ from that of most other states. This was (and probably still is) the discrepancy between foreign and domestic policies, between the course of the ship of state and of the government of the ship. During the dreadful years of the purges Russian foreign policy in the 1930s was receptive to offers of international cooperation against "aggression"; Stalin's foreign commissar Maxim Litvinov, friendly to the Western powers, approved the idea and the phrase "collective security." In 1933 Hitler made Germany abandon the League of Nations; in 1934 the Soviet Union (after many years of excoriating the League as an institution of capitalist imperialism) joined it. In 1935 Moscow signed alliances with Czechoslovakia and with France; in 1936 Stalin chose to send arms and advisers to the leftist Spanish Republic besieged by Franco, who was armed and supported by Mussolini and Hitler. Meanwhile, Communists abroad were ordered to join (and, where possible, direct) "popular fronts," allying themselves with any and every opponent of "Fascism"* throughout the world — while there was nothing even remotely resembling such a policy within the Soviet Union; indeed, the contrary.

By 1938 and 1939 many people (including Winston Churchill) were convinced that the time had come to invite the Soviet Union into an alliance with the Western democracies, threatened as both were by Hitler. That seemed to be a rational and logical course, surely for the West; and perhaps — one would think — for Russia too.

But Stalin did not see things that way.

2

We do not know (and probably will never know) whether there were secret contacts between Stalin and Hitler before 1939; whatever evidence there is remains fragmentary and unreliable.† What we know is something that has not been

* It is significant that *Fascism* and *Fascists* were the terms used within the Soviet Union (and thoughtlessly adopted by its supporters abroad) to designate its adversaries: the more accurate terms *National Socialists* or *Nazis* were prohibited, it seems on orders from Stalin, as early as 1931–1932.

†What we know is that in early 1934 and again in 1937 two minor Soviet officials, well-known to Stalin (first Abel Yenukidze and then David Kandelaki), were sent to Berlin with the ostensible task to seek an extension of German-Soviet commercial relations but also to inquire about the

sufficiently recognized: Stalin's respect and admiration for Germany.* To Anthony Eden, who in March 1935 visited Moscow, Stalin said: "Such a great people as the Germans would have to break loose from the chains of Versailles." And: "The Germans are a great and courageous people. We never forget this."† And now to this came added his respect for and, yes, admiration of Hitler. We know that he was impressed by Hitler's swift elimination of his potential adversaries within his own party in June 1934 ("the night of the thousand knives"); there is some evidence to the effect that it influenced Stalin to proceed with the purges of his own party. In any event, he was impressed by Hitler's successes and by his mass support from Germans of all classes.

He was not impressed by the inclination of British and French politicians and of their governments to seek an alliance with him. On 10 March 1939 he addressed the Congress of the Party (the first one since 1934, when the former practice of annual Congresses had been abandoned and when the mass purges began). The Soviet Union wished to maintain "peaceful, close, and friendly" relations with every power, including Germany. Russia would not "pull the chestnuts

---

chances for more than that. Kandelaki was quite close to Stalin; between 1935 and 1937 he saw Stalin eighteen times, which was very unusual. He stayed long in Berlin. His reports were inaccurate and unintelligent (something that, not incidentally, was so too for the dispatches of many Soviet diplomats). Later he was arrested and shot.

* His very adopted name derives from the Russian transliteration of the German word (Stahl) for steel.

† Nekrich, "22 June 1941," 90.

from the fire" for France and Britain,* meaning that Stalin would not allow them to embroil Russia in a war against Germany. Yet a week after Stalin's speech came a veritable revolution in British public opinion and foreign policy. Hitler had broken his word at Munich and marched into Prague. His next target was Poland. The British and French governments, hoping to deter him from war, were now willing to give a guarantee to Poland. Stalin showed little interest in the resolution finally shown by London and Paris; he saw that Hitler's object now was the elimination of Poland — something from which he, too, could eventually profit. He now told his close-mouthed ambassador in Berlin to speak out. On 17 April, Alexei Merekalov called at the German Foreign Ministry, where he said: "Ideological differences" need not be "a stumbling block" to better and better Russian-German relations. "Soviet Russia had not exploited the present friction between German and the Western democracies, nor did she desire to do so." Then Merekalov took the train to Moscow, reporting to Stalin. A fortnight later, on 4 May, Stalin

* These chestnuts then became a frequent item on the menu of diplomatic rhetoric. (The phrase "pulling the chestnuts from the fire" had often been used by Russian critics of Britain and France during World War I.) Hitler resorted to the same phrase three weeks after Stalin, in his speech at Wilhelmshaven on 1 April 1939: "Anyone who declares himself to be ready to pull the chestnuts out of the fire for the Great Powers must be aware that he might burn his fingers in the process." On 17 May, Ribbentrop told the papal nuncio Cesare Orsenigo in Berlin: "Russia is not disposed to pull the chestnuts from the fire for Britain." *Actes et documents,* 1:152.

dismissed Litvinov, his foreign commissar, proponent of "collective security," and put Molotov in Litvinov's place. One cannot improve on Churchill's summary of what that meant: "The eminent Jew [Litvinov], the target of German antagonism, was flung aside for the time being like a broken tool, and, without being allowed a word of explanation, was bundled off the world stage to obscurity, a pittance, and police supervision. Molotov, little known outside Russia, became Commissar for Foreign Affairs, in the closest confederacy with Stalin. . . . There was in fact only one way in which he was now likely to move. He had always been favourable to an agreement with Hitler."*

This was not lost on Hitler. But he remained cautious (except, as we had seen, allowing to drop a few hints to Paris and London that he may yet be "forced" to make a deal with Stalin). Stalin was cautious, too, and even more secretive than Hitler. But then he also found himself suddenly in a very good position. For the first time since the Bolshevik revolution, Russia's friendship was desired and courted by the European great powers. The Chamberlain government, too, was somewhat cautious, albeit pressed by British opinion (and by Churchill). The British and French governments were slow in sending a military mission to Moscow, in order to explore and perhaps prepare a military alliance with the Soviet Union. They have been criticized for their hum-

* Churchill, *Gathering Storm,* 366.

drum efforts ever since. These criticisms, though not un-justified, miss the mark. Stalin (together with his wooden toady Molotov) had no desire to ally himself with the Western democracies and consequently bear the brunt of an enormous war against Germany. In 1939 Stalin preferred Hitler to Chamberlain. Thereafter, until late — very late, to the night of 22–23 June 1941 — he preferred Hitler to Churchill.

That is not speculation or an analysis post facto. It was evident from the suddenly dramatic development of the negotiations in August 1939. In his few meetings with the British and French missions, Molotov was impassible and un-movable — as a French diplomat said in anger, he sat there like a bump on a log, while the German ambassador found it significant to tell Berlin that, even beyond the prospect of agreeable negotiations, "Herr Molotov was quite unusually compliant and candid" — which was obviously what Stalin had told him to do. And now the drama suddenly accelerated. It was now Hitler who chose to hurry. He had made up his mind to invade Poland on the 26th. That had to be preceded by the great diplomatic coup: the signing of a nonaggression treaty with the Soviet Union. Stalin requested that the signing occur around the 27th, when Ribbentrop could come to Moscow. Hitler requested the 22nd or the 23rd. Letters were exchanged between him and Stalin, who agreed on the 23rd. There are two remarkable matters in these exchanges on the highest level. The text of the German-Soviet nonaggression pact was drafted by Stalin and Molotov, not by Hitler and

Ribbentrop; it was precise, and entirely acceptable to the Germans. Even more important, it was Moscow that suggested that, in addition to the nonaggression treaty, there ought to be a secret protocol, establishing the "spheres of interest" of the two powers, in essence the division of eastern Europe between them. Hitler agreed; he gave a free hand to his foreign minister to deal with that, or with anything else.

Less than a few hours after his landing in Moscow, Ribbentrop, stiff, was sped to the Kremlin, where Stalin awaited him, smiling and evidently happy. There was not a single hitch during their talks, or about the careful wording of the treaty instruments they signed. There was an unusual banquet toward the end of the great visit, with much champagne, with the customary Russian practice of toasts, among them one memorable one. Stalin spontaneously rose and lifted his glass: "I know how much the German nation loves its Führer; I should therefore drink to the health of this great man."* At that very moment beyond the walls of the Kremlin, beyond the iron curtain of the Soviet Union's borders, within and beyond the barbed wires of German concentra-

---

* There is a photograph of their jovial meeting, in which Stalin holds a cigarette in his left hand. Hitler ordered the photo retouched: he said that at such a great occasion there must be no informal picture of a principal statesman holding a cigarette. Next day Stalin bid farewell to Ribbentrop with these words: "The Soviet government takes this new treaty very seriously and gives its word of honor that the Soviet Union will never betray its partner." (About Hitler's — alleged, and unusual — use of "word of honor" see the Appendix, p. 149.)

tion camps, lived and struggled millions of Communists (and their sympathizers), admiring and hoping in Stalin.

The pact did not mean that Stalin and Hitler had suddenly and entirely dropped their ideologies. For Stalin the cause of international Communism had moved ever farther to the back of his mind. Yet there was (and still is) one explanation of why Stalin chose this pact with Hitler, an attribution of his motives as a Communist. He wanted to keep the Soviet Union out of the swiftly approaching world war; but also because such a great European war would eventually strengthen the cause of international Communism; at a certain point the Soviet Union could rake up the ruins of Europe and surge triumphant into a continent devastated by war. The attribution of this plan to Stalin — convincing to anti-Communists throughout the world then and even now — was documented by a text of a secret speech that he had allegedly made to the Politburo on 19 August, explaining and justifying his coming pact with Hitler. The text somehow trickled through to the West and was published first in a reputable French newspaper in November 1939. Countless writers and historians have referred to it ever since. Only recently has it been proved that the entire document is a forgery.*

---

* Slutsch, "Stalins 'Kriegszenario' 1939." Also: most members of the Politburo were told nothing before 21–22 August. Nikita Khrushchev and Kliment Voroshilov were told to go hunting. When Khrushchev prodded Stalin's secretary why in the world Ribbentrop was coming to Moscow, A. Poskrebyshev said that Stalin and Molotov would inform him.

3

Stalin was pleased by the very fact of his partnership with Hitler* and by its prospects, which were territorial: a reconquest of those eastern European lands, former possessions of the Russian empire, that Stalin's predecessor Lenin had lost. This is not a speculative explanation, it is there in some of his own words as well as Molotov's, including the latter's reminiscences half a century later. The cause of Communism now receded into the background, kept on a very low simmer, but it was still there. He was cunning enough to keep certain assets in reserve.† And while the last great wave of the purges receded in March 1939, the brutal practice of disposing of all kinds of potential opponents (nearly all of them innocent) went on, now under the leadership of his secret police chief Lavrent Beria. But the historical argument should not be about the proportions of the mix, Ideologue or Statesman. The compound (not a mix) was that of a Caucasian chieftain and a peasant tsar. What is not arguable is that, latest by 1939, he saw himself more and more as a statesman. As he

* So was Hitler. Molotov spoke on 31 August 1939: "Today we are no longer opponents, a turning point in the history of Europe — and not only Europe." Hitler on 1 September: "I can underwrite Herr Molotov's speech, word by word."

† Example: unlike other Jews and "cosmopolitans" who were killed or imprisoned, Litvinov and Aleksandr Lozovsky were spared, the latter kept as a middle-rank official in the Foreign Commissariat (but then executed in 1952).

himself saw it, this brought him great, very great advantages — for a time. Eventually this very self-assurance turned out to be an enormous handicap, culminating on 22 June 1941, when it brought him and his country to the verge of an enormous catastrophe.

But before we trace his decisions and the course of events, we ought to take a last look at his mental evolution — that is, at the mutation of his ideas. For after his recognition of the supreme importance of the state came his recognition of the prime importance of nations and of nationalism. That was in essence an even more fundamental departure from Marxism than was his emphasis on the primacy of the state, because — this was perhaps the worst shortcoming of Marx's and Engels's dogmatic speculations — they largely ignored nations and nationalism, which almost never figured in their writings. But now Stalin saw (as had Mussolini and Hitler decades before him) that international socialism was largely a mirage: perhaps employable here and there because of its adherents, but so much weaker than nationalism. This recognition, besides and beneath his geopolitical calculations, was the main reason for his admiration of Hitler, for the latter's stupendous achievement of national unity. The Communist International still resided in Moscow, staffed by pensioners who had survived the purges, living at ever lower levels on the edges of the Stalinist bureaucracy. Stalin found it necessary, rather than useful, to talk to its head Georgi Dimitrov from time to time; but the Comintern mattered less and less, in the end hardly at all. There is a — to my mind, very revealing—statement he made in April 1941 to Dimitrov: "The International was formed in Marx's time in the expectation of imminent international revolution. The Comintern, too, was formed in such a period in Lenin's time. Today the *national* tasks of the various countries have priority. . . . Do not cling to what was the rule *yesterday*. Take strict account of the new conditions that have arisen."* In July 1940 an article by Marx's friend and patron Engels, "On the Foreign Policy of Russian Tsarism," was about to be published in the leading Russian Communist periodical, *Bolshevik*. Stalin forbade it. He wrote in a note: "Aggressive vileness is not a monopoly of Russian tzars. . . . In attacking Tsarist foreign policy [Engels] deprives it from any trust."†

He was surprised and impressed by the speed of the German campaign in Poland. So he had to advance the Russian occupation of eastern Poland sooner than he had expected. That occurred on 17 September. There were no real incidents when the advancing Russian troops came up against their German allies all along the division line. Ten days later Ribbentrop flew to Moscow again, to make adjustments on that dreadful map, exchanging territories, among them assigning Lithuania to the Soviet sphere. That meeting between Ribbentrop and Molotov and Stalin was another happy occasion. On 31 October, Molotov, on Stalin's orders, made one of the most contemptible speeches in his long and

---

* Dimitrov, *Diary,* 20 April 1941.
† Volkogonov, *Stalin,* 552.

contemptible career, describing Poland as an unnatural cancerous growth on the map.*

To Stalin the suggestive and yet imprecise phrase "spheres of interest" meant an entirely free hand over what had fallen to his side across the new German-Soviet border. So he and Molotov forced the unfortunate envoys of the Baltic states in Moscow to accept the stationing of Russian garrisons and naval establishments on their territories. The Estonians, Latvians, Lithuanians had to accept, hoping that despite these military concessions their — minimal — civic independence could prevail. Farther to their south the Soviet-occupied portions of Poland were simply annexed to the Soviet Union. Having dealt with the Baltic states, Stalin almost immediately turned on Finland, also allotted to his "sphere of interest." Again the main issue was territorial and military, a demand for frontier changes and for at least one Russian naval base. There was at least one reason for the former: the Finnish frontier after 1920 ran very close to Leningrad. The Finns knew that; they were not altogether unreasonable; yet it was soon evident that what Stalin wanted was their consent to come within his sphere of interest — that is, empire. He, rather than the Finns, broke off negotiations. He ordered the faking of an "incident" along the Finnish-Russian border; using that as a pretext, on 30 November he went to war with Finland.

---

* Goebbels in his diaries: "Very strong in our favor. He said everything we may have wanted." *Tagebücher,* 3:628. On the night of 10–11 November, thirty-nine German aircraft dropped two million pamphlets with Molotov's speech over French lines.

This was a war between two states: an enormous and brutal Russia, a bitter and brave Finland. Yet Stalin gave it an ideological packaging. Employing a gaggle of exiled Finnish Communists whose "government" he established on the Finnish-Russian border, he used the pretext of assisting that "people's government" against the "reactionary" regime in Helsinki. But this war soon developed into a sorry business for the Russians. Their army and their air force performed miserably. It took nearly three months for the Russians to summon enough might to break through the main defense line of their so much smaller opponent. By early March the Finns were constrained to sign a peace treaty. That paper, significantly, contained not a word about the "Finnish people's government," the pretext and the packaging with which the Winter War had begun. Finland lost some land, an important town, and a naval base, but her independent existence remained, alone among the lands in Stalin's sphere of interest. (Something similar would occur with Finland after the Second World War and throughout the so-called cold war.)

The lamentable Russian performance during the Winter War impressed the entire world, including, of course, Germany's generals. (There was also a fleeting moment when Britain and France came close to risking a marginal war against the Soviet Union.) Stalin convoked a meeting of his military commanders in April to discuss their shortcomings during the Winter War. The results were not entirely conclusive; some people were dismissed, others were not. Something much greater, something much more spectacular was happening on the world scene. In April, Hitler marched into Denmark and Norway; his Germans easily beat the British out of the latter country. On 10 May his armies lunged forward in the West. Holland surrendered after four days, Belgium after eighteen, France in less than six weeks, while Britain fought on, but how? and for how long? Stalin instructed Molotov to send a fulsome congratulation to Hitler ("the brilliant success of the German Army"). At the same time Stalin decided to cash in. He ordered (on the day Paris fell) the full incorporation of the Baltic states into his empire. He sent some of his worst satraps to their capitals: Vladimir Dekanozov to Lithuania, Andrei Vishinsky to Latvia, Andrei Zhdanov to Estonia. Truckloads of Russian infantry and tanks rumbled into these luckless flatlands. Ten days later Stalin ordered a sudden ultimatum to Rumania, demanding the surrender of (once Russian) Bessarabia, at the same time adding another slice of northwestern Rumania to his empire (northern Bukovina, a portion not mentioned in the secret protocol). Hitler was now disturbed by Stalin's interpretation of what "spheres of interest" meant. His eye and mind began to wander eastward, thinking about what a German conquest of Russia might mean in this war.

Churchill sensed this. On 25 June he wrote a letter to Stalin — a great state paper in the history of twentieth-century diplomacy. The essence of his letter was this: Germany has now conquered all of Europe, or most of it. There are two of us remaining on the edges of the continent. We British will keep fighting until Hitler's might is broken. I do not expect you to side with us, surely not now, but don't you think that we ought to exchange views, at least from time to time? Churchill did not expect an answer. There was, of course, none. The letter went to the recently appointed British ambassador to the Soviet Union, Sir Stafford Cripps, an unfortunate appointment. It took Cripps almost a week to get an interview with Stalin. Before that Molotov kept refusing to see him. After meeting with Cripps, Stalin told Molotov to let the fact and the content of Churchill's message be known to the Germans, to assure Hitler that he, Stalin, would have no truck with Churchill.

Stalin thought — as did most people during that deadly summer of 1940 — that Hitler was planning to invade England. None of his agents had yet known of Hitler's declaration to his generals on 31 July, to prepare for an eventual invasion of Russia. But there began a gradual increase of German troop units in Poland. By the end of September, Stalin knew that there would be no German invasion of England that year. He also knew of the Tripartite Pact of Germany, Italy, Japan, with its unusual clause appeasing the Soviet Union. Now he thought that the time was ripe for another great arrangement, extending the spheres of interest with Hitler, the first step of which must be sending Molotov to visit Hitler and Ribbentrop in Berlin. At the same time Stalin was disturbed by certain developments in his neighborhood. Finland had been allotted to his sphere of interest; he had let a diminished Finland remain independent; but now, in August 1940, German missions began to arrive in Finland. Other unpleasant developments came in the Balkans.* By August–September 1940, German troops were moving across Hungary into Rumania, attaching the latter to the German sphere. Was it not reasonable to request that at least Bulgaria, a traditionally Russophile state and nation, be permitted to join the Russian sphere?† There were carefully worded Russian diplomatic protests against the unilateral German behavior in Rumania. There was another Russian attempt for a sphere-of-interest agreement with Mussolini in the Balkans. Nothing came of these. But then their significance paled before the prospect of a greater scope: a further division of Eurasia through an agreement between Hitler and himself.‡

We have seen that this did not happen; that, instead of hearing out Molotov's argument, Hitler was irritated by him, especially by Molotov's harping on Bulgaria and Finland. Now Stalin chose not to disavow Molotov but to reverse the order of the priorities on which the latter had insisted in Berlin, that the Finnish and Bulgarian issues be

* Yet on 23 August an article in *Pravda* celebrated and extolled the first anniversary of the Hitler-Stalin Pact: "one of the most important documents in the history of international relations in our era."

† In this respect, too, Stalin acted in perfect accord with what had been once tsarist diplomacy. He established diplomatic relations with Yugoslavia in June 1940, assuring his support to the Serbian monarchy; in October and November he offered his support to the tsar of Bulgaria.

‡ Stalin gave fourteen directives to Molotov before the latter traveled to Berlin. During his negotiations Molotov sought, and got, further directives from Stalin (on 13 November).

settled before turning to the larger issues. Now Stalin ordered Molotov to prepare a draft of a much greater scope: a division of Europe, Asia, Africa among Germany, Italy, Japan, and Russia into spheres of influence. Just as in the August 1939 pact, Stalin's new draft included secret protocols: the German spheres of influence would include central Africa, the Italian one northern Africa, the Japanese one southeastern Asia, the Soviet Union's south of its present empire, in the Middle East in the direction of the Indian Ocean. A second secret protocol called for a joint effort to make Turkey conform to the wishes of Germany and Russia. On 26 November, Molotov gave the German ambassador to Moscow and the new Russian ambassador to Berlin (Dekanozov) a more extensive and precise version of that draft. The text began by referring to the statement about a world-wide four-power pact such as Ribbentrop had mentioned in Berlin, which the Soviet government was now prepared to accept. This more detailed draft included five secret protocols: one about Bulgaria,* one about Finland, one about Russian-Japanese relations, one about Turkey, one about control of the Turkish Strairs: in sum, the division of the Balkans, and the prospective division of most of Eurasia.

There was no reaction from Berlin, not even confirmation of its receipt. But there was no sign that Hitler's indifference

---

* It added—significantly—that if Bulgaria would accept a mutual-assistance pact with the Soviets, then the latter would not object to Bulgaria's joining the Tripartite Treaty, which then the Soviet Union might join too.

to this grand offer weighed heavily on Stalin's mind. The Soviet press went on publishing occasional Wehrmacht communiqués. Important imports of oil, rubber, and other strategic raw materials from the Soviet Union to Germany were delivered punctually; indeed, their volume kept increasing, as recorded by the respective German agencies in Berlin.* Meanwhile, the Russians got nowhere in the Balkans. On 1 March the German army moved into Bulgaria. Yugoslavia was next; yet as we have seen, the Belgrade coup d'état was a hitch, albeit a temporary one; and Stalin felt compelled to make at least a gesture, a "nonaggression" pact with the unfortunate Yugoslavs. But 1941 was not 1914, and Hitler's armies overran and broke up Yugoslavia in a model Blitzkrieg. And now the accumulation of events led to a startling episode in the course of Stalinite diplomacy (if the ancient and honorable word *diplomacy* applies to such episodes at all).

On 12 April the Japanese Matsuoka stopped in Moscow on his way back to the Far East. He and Stalin signed a nonaggression treaty. There were unusual circumstances at that

---

* One small evidence of Stalin's and Molotov's insistence on territory involved the case of Suwalki, a minuscule triangle of land that according to the September 1939 arrangement lay on the German side of the partition line. After lengthy negotiations the Germans agreed to incessant Russian demands, transferring these few muddy acres to the Russians in exchange for a sum of $7.5 million (more than the tsar's empire had been paid in 1867 for all of Alaska). On 22–23 June a German army moved across Suwalki in a matter of hours.

ceremony. It took place at lunch, not at dinner, an unusually long lunch with much drinking and jollity, to which the Japanese were evidently unaccustomed; even the dour Molotov was deep in his cups. A parade of automobiles took the Japanese to the railroad station, where they would board the Trans-Siberian Express for the long journey eastward. But then it was announced that the departure of the train would be delayed by an hour. Suddenly there appeared another covey of big black automobiles, wherefrom emerged no lesser personages than Stalin and Molotov, smiling and stumbling. Murmur and commotion rose among the assembled officials and the diplomatic corps, among them the spare and elegant ambassador of Germany. Stalin was evidently looking for him; he ambled up to Schulenburg, trying to put his short arms around the ambassador's tall shoulders, and said rather loudly: "We must remain friends and [you] must now do everything to that end!" Then he embraced the German military attaché: "We will remain friends with you — in any event!" His gestures had all the subtlety of a bear trying to tango. The Germans were much impressed.* Hitler was not.

---

*NSR, 324. The Japanese were beside themselves with excitement. How unprecedented! Such honor! Their ambassador to Moscow, also drunk, jumped up and down, screaming "Thanks!" "Thanks!" Saying farewell, his foreign minister addressed Stalin as "Your highness." A generation later Henry Kissinger wrote that "Richelieu or Bismarck would have had no difficulty understanding [Stalin's] strategy." Gorodetsky, *Grand Delusion,* 199. Oh well. This was not the world of Richelieu or of Bismarck . . .

4

A clue to what followed is no longer Stalin's statesmanship; it is his enduring faith in Hitler. Report after report arrived in Moscow, not only about the increasing mass of German divisions in Poland but about Hitler's decision to invade Russia, some of the reports mentioning mid-June. That Stalin was reluctant to believe them is an understatement; he did not credit them at all. He did not, indeed, he could not believe that Hitler would choose a war with him while his Germany was still at war with England. A two-front war Hitler would not want.

On the evening of 4 May, Stalin and the Politburo decided to elevate him to the prime ministership of the state. (Before that he was officially nothing more than the first secretary of the Party.) This was announced to the Soviet peoples and to the world two days later. The meaning of this was not lost on Schulenburg, who summed it up again and again. Stalin has now "taken over the supreme power of the state . . . and the two strongest men in the Soviet Union — Stalin and Molotov — hold positions which are decisive for the foreign policy of the Soviet Union. . . . This foreign policy is, after all, directed at the avoidance of a conflict with Germany. [This] is proved by the attitude taken by the Soviet Government during the last few weeks and by the tone of the Soviet press."*

On the night before the announcement of his prime minis-

* *NSR,* 344.

tership, Stalin made a speech the contents of which have been debated ever since. The occasion was a banquet in the Kremlin for the graduates of sixteen military academies of the Red Army. There exists no exact text of this speech; there are at least four or five versions of it. A succinct summary of the speech was Dimitrov's: "There is no defense without offense. The army must be educated in the spirit of offensives. We must be prepared for war." Stalin spoke, for once, about the German army. According to one version he said that the Germans were not invincible after all; according to another, that the German army was very strong. Unlike his alleged speech of 19 August 1939, these versions are not forgeries. But here we run up against what are now widespread, and sometimes fabricated, allegations. Stalin's speech has been employed by those who claim that he was preparing an attack against Germany in July 1941 but that Hitler preempted him: that in sum, Hitler's invasion of Russia on 22 June was a preventive move. This propaganda was started as early as 1977 by David Irving, an admirer of Hitler, in his book *Hitler's War,* citing one or two entirely irrelevant frames of microfilm for his "evidence." Ten years later more reputable German historians turned to a more subtle attempt to explain Hitler, at least partially, advancing two arguments: first, that Communism was as bad, if not worse, than Nazism and that the Holocaust was in many ways a response to the Gulag; second, that Stalin was about to attack Germany in 1941.*

---

*That Stalin was about to attack Germany in 1941 was taken up by

There was no such plan. This is now the consensus of most serious historians.* Moreover, Stalin — no matter what was his tone on 5 May in his speech to the officer-candidates — made yet another move to impress Hitler with his friendship. On 10 May he ordered the rupture of Soviet relations with the Belgian and Dutch and Norwegian and Greek and Yugoslav governments, and ordered the expulsion of their legations from Moscow. Yet even more important was something that developed behind the scenes. It involved two men, the respective ambassadors in Moscow and in Berlin: Schulenburg, that most impressive German aristocrat,† and Deka-

---

Günther Gillessen in the reputable *Frankfurter Allgemeine,* by an Austrian, Ernst Topitsch, also by the German military historian Joachim Hoffman, by one of Hitler's biographers (Werner Maser), and even by an American (R. C. Raack). These writers got substantial support from Viktor Suvarov (pseudonym of a Soviet defector), from the very dubious former secret police official Pavel Sudoplatov, also by Russian writers and historians Vladimir Nevezhin, Shaptalnov, Metyukhov. In the case of some of them the purpose of their denigration of Stalin (and there is plenty to denigrate there) has been, alas, an ingenious mitigation of Hitler — again, that his invasion of Russia in June was but a reaction to Stalin's plans to attack him in July.

* True, for some time Soviet military doctrine declared that in case of war there was an immediate need to move across the borders of the Soviet Union into enemy territory. (Which was not what the Soviet army did in 1938 and 1939, defeating two armed Japanese attempts to break into Soviet Mongolia.) Also, alarmed by the obvious and rapid increase of German forces at the border, on 15 May, Generals Georgi Zhukov and Semyon Timoshenko presented a plan for a preventive offensive across it. Stalin rejected it, instantly.

† Twenty-seven years before, at the outbreak of the First World War, the young Schulenburg had written to a Russian lady friend how "unnecessary" this war between Germany and Russia was.

nozov, an unimpressive former secret policeman but now Stalin's principal envoy to Hitler.

On 28 April, Hitler received Schulenburg in Berlin. He gave him not more than half an hour. Schulenburg told him that Stalin's relations with Britain were not improving; to the contrary, Stalin wanted to demonstrate his intention to collaborate with Germany; the Yugoslav episode no longer mattered; he was convinced that Stalin was prepared to make even more concessions to Germany. Hitler was not convinced; he said little, save a last rapid throwaway remark at the end: "One more thing, Count Schulenburg, I do not intend a war against Russia."* Schulenburg was far from being convinced of that; he returned to Moscow with darkest premonitions in his mind. Dekanozov was in Moscow at the same time, reporting to Stalin. Stalin made him stand next to him atop Red Square at the 1 May celebrations — another signal to Hitler, no doubt. And now (especially impressed by Stalin's elevation to the top of his government on 5 May) Schulenburg, in desperation, took matters into his hand. He met Dekanozov three times before the latter's return to Berlin. He spoke at some length about what could and must be done to avert war between their two countries. He was not authorized to do so, he knew that, and yet he went very far. In the end he suggested that Stalin write a personal letter to Hitler. Stalin and Molotov consulted with

* Hilger, *Incompatible Allies*, 106. Four days later Hitler ordered a gift of 200,000 Reichsmarks to help repair Schulenburg's country estate.

Dekanozov; they told him to go ahead with this plan of a letter.*

5

More than a dozen books and many more articles now contain texts and lists of secret, and sometimes not secret, intelligence coming to Moscow during the last two months before the German invasion. Many of their items have been quoted by various writers, historians, archivists, novelists, and amateurs, as well as academics, during the past two decades, due to the partial (and of course incomplete) availability of Russian archives.† Telling or dramatic or shocking (especially in retrospect) as many of these secret reports were, it may be sufficient to sum them up here, mostly according to their provenances and sources.‡

They came, first of all, from statesmen, the very leaders of other great powers. On 17 April, Churchill, impatient, took up his pen. He wrote a long message to Stalin, informing him what British intelligence knew of the German military concentration against Russia. When his ambassador Cripps seemed to have been dilatory in passing this important note

---

*Was there such a letter? Was there such a correspondence? I shall deal with this sequence of events in some detail in the Appendix.

† An early and very honorable attempt was made by A. M. Nekrich, in a lecture in Moscow in 1965 (since reprinted).

‡ See in detail Murphy, *What Stalin Knew;* also *1941 g.*

to Molotov and Stalin, Churchill was angry. He should not have been: His letter made no difference. Stalin went on, trusting Hitler. A month earlier, on 20 March, Roosevelt told his highly intelligent Undersecretary of State Sumner Welles to call in the Soviet ambassador Konstantin Umansky and give him information about the German massing of troops in Poland. On 15 April the American ambassador in Moscow, Laurence Steinhardt, said much the same thing to Lozovsky in the Russian Foreign Ministry. Stalin's comment was that these were nothing but Anglo-American attempts to provoke a war between Germany and Russia from which London and Washington would profit. (The British ambassador Cripps, disconcerted by the Russians' behavior, flew back to London via Stockholm twelve days before 22 June; he did not get back to Moscow until the 25th.) The Russian ambassador in London, Ivan Maisky, who formerly had had a good relationship with Churchill, was now afraid of Stalin and therefore noncommittal and useless. Churchill ordered Alexander Cadogan, the permanent undersecretary of the Foreign Office, to call in Maisky on 10 June. Cadogan told Maisky to sit down and get pencil and paper. "On the instruction of His Majesty's Government," he read him item and item of what intelligence London had about the coming German invasion: "The Prime Minister asks you urgently to communicate all these data to the Soviet Government." It had no effect. From faraway China came a report from Chiang Kai-Shek, putting the date of the German attack at 21 June.

Almost without exception the Russian ambassadors and ministers in the various capital cities of the world were reluctant — or, more precisely, afraid* — to tell Stalin what he, more and more obviously, did not wish to hear. That kind of semi-Oriental subservience to the great khan or tsar had a very damaging effect on the accumulating, and often quite accurate, reports of agents who worked abroad for Russian military intelligence. Stalin had dismissed the sometimes outspoken and reliable head of military intelligence in July 1940 (Ivan I. Proskurov was imprisoned later and then was shot) with a man, Filipp I. Golikov, who, almost till the very day of the German invasion, agreed, or at least pretended to agree, with Stalin. A report from a Czech agent as early as April asserted a German invasion in mid-June. Stalin's note on the margin: "English provocateur! Investigate!" And that was but one source whose information corresponded almost exactly with the repeated messages from the later-so-famous Richard Sorge in Tokyo: "Germany will begin a war against the Soviet Union in the middle of June" (on 5 May); "I repeat, nine armies, 150 divisions will begin an offensive at dawn on June 22" (on 13 June). Stalin dismissed Sorge: a lightweight, "a little shit."†

---

*One example: the Soviet minister in Bulgaria, about whom his British colleague wrote: "a rather loutish creature, obviously terrified of committing himself."

†Murphy, *What Stalin Knew*, 87 et seq. Sorge was arrested by the Japanese secret police in late 1941 and executed three years later. In the 1960s he was declared a Hero of the Soviet Union.

Another intelligence apparatus was that of the state secret police (the NKVD, headed by Beria), often less reliable than military intelligence, and weighted down by the handicap of spineless personnel: for example, A. Z. Kobulov, the main agent posted in the Berlin embassy after the Hitler-Stalin pact, who was not only stupid but who relied on fake information provided him by a German double agent. Yet there was plenty of evidence coming from other sources, too — for example, from a bitter opponent of Hitler in the German Air Ministry,* one of whose friends slipped information to an American diplomat in Berlin (Sam E. Woods). The head of the secret police foreign intelligence operation, Pavel Fitin, was no fool. He felt compelled to send an important report from one of these top German sources to Merkulov, the commissar of state security, who put it on Stalin's desk. "All preparations by Germany for an armed attack on the Soviet Union have been completed; the blow can be expected at any time." Stalin wrote on the margin: "Comrade Merkulov, you can send your 'source' from the headquarters of German aviation to his —— ing mother. This is not a 'source' but a 'Dezinformator.'"† He wrote this on 17 June, Tuesday, less than five full days before Hitler's invasion was to begin.

This kind of evidence, damning Stalin's unwillingness to listen, is impressive. However, we must keep in mind that

---

* Rudolf von Scheliha, also Harro Schultze-Boysen and Arvid Harnack, found out and executed in 1942. Cf. two of their important and accurate reports on 19 May and 16 June, *1941g.*, docs. 493 and 570.

† Murphy, *What Stalin Knew*, xv.

secret intelligence includes hundreds of straws in the wind, implying intentions rather than acts. But then there was plenty of increasingly massive evidence not only of intentions but of acts. There were almost one thousand miles of the frontier between the Soviet Union and Germany and the latter's allies, in East Prussia, Poland, Hungary, Rumania. Only a few weeks before June, joint German-Soviet border commissions had surveyed and marked the exact lines separating them, especially when the frontier line did not consist of a river. Athwart the flat, green, melancholy Polish plains it was impossible to conceal or even to obscure what was going on on the German side, with its accumulation of masses of troops and of many thousands of military engines. Besides, as happens at almost every border, however guarded, there was always a small trickle of men and women filtering across, for whatever purposes, some of them agents or saboteurs. The special Soviet agency of Border Troops reported the arrest of suspicious persons: their numbers rose five- or six-fold in the first months of 1941. By mid-June there was direct evidence of saboteurs crossing over to damage Byelorussian and Ukrainian rail lines. On 16 June the first deserter from a German army unit came over: but his report was disbelieved.

Even more telling is the case of German overflights, obvious violations of the otherwise so rigidly observed Soviet principle of the sovereignty of the state. As early as March 1940 Stalin told Beria to issue an order: "In case of violations of the Soviet-German frontier by German aircrafts or balloons do not open fire."* Also: in case of border violations, "strictly see to it that bullets do not fall on German territory." By March and April 1941, there were so many German over-flights that a few carefully worded and anxious diplomatic protests were made to German authorities in Berlin and Moscow. They did not matter, because Stalin ordered no interference, no antiaircraft fire against German warplanes, no matter how far they were flying over Soviet territories. In essence, he gave German aerial reconnaissance a free hand.† "Do *not* open fire!" Disaster was the result: on 22 June the Luftwaffe destroyed close to one half of the Russian air force, airplanes parked on their fields or in their hangars.

At seven on the evening of 13 June, Friday, megaphones in cities and towns of the Soviet Union blared forth the text of an official (TASS) communiqué. An hour or so later Molotov himself called on the German ambassador, giving him the text. Next morning all daily newspapers in the Soviet Union were told to print that text on their first pages:

Even before the return of the English Ambassador Cripps to London, but especially after his return, there have been widespread rumors of "an impending war between the U.S.S.R. and Germany" in the English and foreign press. These rumors allege:

* Murphy, *What Stalin Knew,* 165.
† Two high-level German informers warned Moscow that these German planes now carried extensive photographic equipment.

1. That Germany supposedly has made various territorial and economic demands on the U.S.S.R. and that at present negotiations are impending between Germany and the U.S.S.R. for the conclusion of a new and closer agreement between them;

2. That the Soviet Union is supposed to have declined these demands and that as a result Germany has begun to concentrate her troops on the frontier of the Soviet Union in order to attack the Soviet Union;

3. That on its side the Soviet Union is supposed to have begun intensive preparations for war with Germany and to have concentrated its troops on the German border.

Despite the obvious absurdity of these rumors, responsible circles in Moscow have thought it necessary, in view of the persistent spread of these rumors, to authorize Tass to state that these rumors are a clumsy propaganda maneuver of the forces arrayed against the Soviet Union and Germany, which are interested in a spread and intensification of the war.

Tass declares that:

1. Germany has addressed no demands to the Soviet Union and has asked for no new closer agreement, and that therefore negotiations cannot be taking place;

2. According to the evidence in the possession of the Soviet Union, both Germany and the Soviet Union are fulfilling to the letter the terms of the Soviet-German Nonaggression Pact, so that in the

opinion of Soviet circles the rumors of the intention of Germany to break the Pact and to launch an attack against the Soviet Union are completely without foundation, while the recent movements of German troops which have completed their operations in the Balkans, to the eastern and northern parts of Germany, must be explained by other motives which have no connection with Soviet-German relations;

3. The Soviet Union, in accordance with its peace policy, has fulfilled and intends to fulfill the terms of the Soviet-German Nonaggression Pact; as a result, all the rumors according to which the Soviet Union is preparing for a war with Germany are false and provocative;

4. The summer calling-up of the reserves of the Red Army which is now taking place and the impending maneuvers mean nothing but a training of the reservists and a check on the operations of the railroad system, which as is known takes place every year; consequently, it appears at least nonsensical to interpret these measures of the Red Army as an action hostile to Germany.*

"Responsible circles": there is at least circumstantial evidence that much of this text was written by Stalin himself. What else was this but a repetition of that scene at the Moscow railway station two months before? And yet things were no longer the same: the Third Reich's army was being made ready; German airplanes, unharmed, flew high and

*NSR, 345–46.

low over Russian airfields; and Hitler now permitted his putative allies, Finns, Rumanians, Hungarians, to be informed that a German war against the Soviet Union was imminent.

Three more days and nights passed. There was no, absolutely no, reaction from Berlin, not even a confirmation of that abject "communiqué" from Moscow.* Stalin remained impassive.† Warnings and reports were now pouring in. Generals Timoshenko and Zhukov tried to impress Stalin, but in vain. They returned to their argument time and time again, again on 18 June in Stalin's office, with members of the Politburo present. Stalin's voice rose to a shout at Zhukov: "Have you come to scare us with war, or do you want a war because you don't have enough medals? If you're going to provoke the Germans on the frontier by moving troops there without our permission, then heads will roll, mark my words!" Stalin slammed the door.‡

It was natural for the Germans to mislead the world, and of course the Russians, as much as was possible. One clever

---

* Cripps having left for London, the British chargé in Moscow (Baggalay) made a protest about the text of the TASS communiqué. It was dismissed. *1941 g*, docs. 522, 562.

† Beria was not. By early June he was convinced that the Germans would attack. Consequently on the night of 14–15 June he ordered "special actions": the deportations of tens of thousands of "unreliable elements" in the Baltic populations — 60,000 Estonians, 36,000 Latvians, 75,000 Lithuanians (respectively, 6, 1.8, and 3.7 percent of the populations).

‡ Gorodetsky, *Grand Delusion*, 299; but his information (from Lev Bezymensky) is not entirely reliable.

scheme was prepared by Goebbels, who on 15 June (the day after the TASS communiqué) ordered and made widely known the confiscation of an edition of the German newspaper that had printed an article suggesting a coming German parachute invasion of England. His purpose was to suggest the potential imminence of such an event. Hitler agreed to this deception. Yet we have also seen that he did little to conceal his real intentions. Meanwhile the German press began to print occasional anti-Soviet articles. On 14 June, Goebbels wrote in his diary: "The Russians are mesmerized by us and they are afraid. . . . The Russians seem not to suspect anything. In any case their military dispositions are just what we would wish: thickly massed, easy to [encircle and] capture."*

Of one matter we may be certain. This was Stalin's consistent distrust of the English. He saw them as prototypical imperialists and capitalists, worse than the Germans whom he respected; he knew much less about England and the English than about Germany and Germans (as was also the case of many others in the Moscow Communist hierarchy). He also believed (and of course there was reason to believe this) that it was a British interest to have a war come between the Third Reich and the Soviet Union; that it was indeed in their interest to provoke it. Hitler knew that too — except that he needed no British provocation to attack and

---

* Goebbels, *Tagebücher*, 668–669. But also: "I esteem the Russians' fighting ability as very low, lower than does the Führer" (695).

crush Russia. We have seen that as late as 18 June, Stalin attributed most, if not all, reports of an imminent German attack to English (or American) provocations. Yet by Thursday, 19 June, he could no longer deny the possibility of what was coming. There was a veritable swarm of German over-flights beyond the western frontiers. Report after report came in. Stalin's daily schedule may be of some interest. He spent all of his nights and some of his days in his dacha at Kuntsevo, outside Moscow (though not far, less than half an hour from the Kremlin in a fast automobile). Usually he came to his Kremlin office in the early afternoons, staying there and working into the wee hours of the morning. Late that Thursday he finally signed an order to conceal and camouflage airplanes and airfields. (It was too little and too late.) That day there was yet another report from an agent in Germany, to the effect that the German attack would begin on Sunday. It was not shown to Stalin. An article in *Pravda* attacked the — temporarily absent — British ambassador: "The Russo-German Pact stands firm, unbroken."* That night and Friday, German ships, many of them unloaded, began to raise their anchors in Soviet ports, putting out to sea for Germany. In Finnish ports fifteen German ships were docked, and ten thousand German troops were reported to have moved into Finland from northern Norway.

Saturday, 21 June, was an unusually warm day. People in Moscow went on with their daily chores. *Rigoletto* and *La*

* Elvin, *Cockney in Moscow*, 53.

Traviata were on the program of the operas. Hundreds of miles to the west, along the long border, there was a rumble of movements. Another German deserter had swum across one of the border rivers, telling about the attack to start in the coming dawn hours. The longest day of the year: sunlight until very late in the evening. Some time after six, on that relentlessly bright summer afternoon, Molotov and others of the Politburo assembled in Stalin's apartment in the Kremlin.

They sat together for another five or six hours (there is some confusion about the exact time in their various reminiscences). Meanwhile the first signals of the war were coming in. Molotov left Stalin's apartment around nine for an hour or so, walking up to his office a few minutes away. For he and Stalin had agreed—finally—to protest to the Germans about that increasing swarm of German flights into Russian airspace. That was the first protest addressed to Berlin from Moscow in many weeks. There was more than that. In Berlin, Dekanozov was told to keep calling at the German Foreign Ministry, but he called largely in vain; his German counterparts restricted their conversation to visa questions. Now Dekanozov was told to see Ribbentrop but was directed instead to his undersecretary, Ernst von Weizsaecker, handing to him the same diplomatic protest note that Molotov was presenting to Schulenburg in the Kremlin. "Herr Dekanozov tried to prolong the conversation somewhat," but Weizsaecker told him, "Not now." In Moscow, Molotov said more. "There were a number of indications that the

German government was dissatisfied with the Soviet government." Rumors were even current that a war was impending between Germany and the Soviet Union. "But why? [Herr Molotov] would appreciate it if I could tell him what brought about the present situation in German-Soviet Russian relations."* Schulenburg replied that he could not answer Molotov's question but that he would transmit his communication to Berlin. Returning to the German embassy, Schulenburg (what bitter thoughts must have coursed through his mind) drafted a summary of his conversation with Molotov and wired it to Berlin, where its arrival was recorded at 2:30 in the morning of 22 June — forty-five minutes before the invasion of the Russian empire was to begin.

After the report of a new German deserter arrived (who, among other things, told the Russian border guards that his unit had been told to prepare crossing the river Bug into Soviet territory in the next few hours), Stalin still proposed caution; he said that the Germans might have sent this man over to provoke us; but now he ordered Generals Timoshenko and Zhukov to come to his office. They and other Politburo men now began to press Stalin to order a general military alert. More alarming news was coming in, about saboteurs who were within the border cutting military telephone and telegraph wires. On the German side of the border Germans were taking down barbed wire and assembling

---

*NSR, 355. Somewhat piteously, Molotov also brought up the Yugoslav episode of April: was that one of the reasons of the German disaffection with Russia? He hoped not, for that was now in the past.

boats and pontoons ready to cross the rivers in front of them. Finally—very late, upon the generals' insistent urging—Stalin and the others agreed to issue a general order: "High Alert. . . . A surprise attack by the Germans on 22–23 June is possible. . . . The attack may start with provocative actions. The task of our troops is not to respond to any provocative actions that might result in serious complications." (The order did not reach the command posts for at least three more hours, again too late). The very ambiguous language of these instructions reflected Stalin's own ambivalence. Around ten, for the first time, he dropped one remark: yes, perhaps war could start tomorrow. According to some accounts, all or most of the Politburo men followed Stalin out of the Kremlin around eleven, everyone driving to his dacha in Kuntsevo. According to Mikoyan, Stalin still "kept reassuring us that Hitler would not begin the war."* According to Molotov, they may even have watched a movie—which they had often done—until shortly before two in the morning. In any event, Stalin went to bed when they left, sometime around two, in the darkest hour of what was (and would be his) shortest night of the year.

* Montefiore, *Stalin,* 358.

PART II

The Twenty-Second of June

CHAPTER FOUR

Berlin

On Sunday morning the people of Germany woke up to learn that they were now at war with Russia. In Berlin the weather was hot and sunny, uncomfortably so. (Goebbels complained in his diary of the warm nights — this was of course before air conditioning.)

It is not easy to reconstruct the reactions of the German people. They were not uniform. The secret "surveys of sentiment" organized by Heinrich Himmler's office stated that people supported the Führer's decision. We may add: by and large, but perhaps not entirely. Contemporaries have used the word *shock*. There were conservative Germans who welcomed Hitler's decision to attack the satanic Communist state in the East (but then those were also people who in

August 1939 did not much object to the pact with Stalin; they saw it as a mark of Hitler's genius of statecraft). Others were inclined to trust the official pretext, that the Red Army had been about to attack Germany. The prospect of a two-front war or memories of Napoleon seemed to bother few. The citizens of Berlin were generally more sophisticated than other Germans; many of them shrugged their shoulders, we may say. There were not many signs of enthusiasm; but the confidence in their armed forces remained strong.

It was different at the front. The reminiscences of many thousands of German soldiers of 21–22 June 1941 tell of their surprise — in some cases incredulity — before the final order to march: what reason was there for a war with the "Ivans"? They would give us most, if not everything, that we may want from them. And indeed there were few signs of preparation for war on the other side, even when in the last daylight hours of Saturday, 21 June, the German preparations had become visible and evident. Shortly before midnight a passenger train bound for Berlin clattered across the big frontier bridge of the Bug near Brest-Litovsk. An hour later came a long freight train, loaded with goods from Russia to Germany. The two red lights of its caboose slowly dimmed and disappeared in the west. Then there was quiet, except — this is common to almost all of the reminiscences — for a veritable symphony of millions of frogs, frogs croaking and carping through the short summer night. At 3:15 A.M. a thousand German cannons broke the half-silence, and fires lit up the predawn sky.

In Berlin, Ribbentrop called for the Russian ambassador to come to his office at 4 A.M. Both men were nervous. Ribbentrop began by stating that "the hostile attitude of the Soviet government toward Germany and the serious threat that Germany saw in the Russian concentration on the eastern border of Germany had forced the Reich to military countermeasures." Dekanozov attempted to explain that the German analysis was "erroneous" and that he regretted this, but Ribbentrop did not let him talk. Then Dekanozov asked Ribbentrop: wasn't there a misunderstanding? "Wasn't there a mistake?" (A question that was, at best, not very dignified and, at worst, pitiful.) Ribbentrop, too, was not his best. He said something to the effect that he personally regretted what had to happen since he had made every effort to stabilize German relations with Russia. (But then Ribbentrop's best was never very good; till the end of his life he remained the rigidest blinkered servant of Hitler.)

And now let us, for the last time, return to Hitler and to his purposes. The still widely accepted explanation is that his motives and purposes* were ideological, primarily and principally so: that this was the war he had always wanted. Many historians have argued this, some Germans among them going so far as to state that until 22 June 1941 Germany fought "a normal European war" and that thereafter that changed (and that Hitler's war against England was "of

---

* Motives and purposes: they are not the same. Modern psychoanalysis as well as much of modern literature confuses or ignores their differences. A motive is a push from one's past; a purpose is a pull of one's future.

secondary importance": Andreas Hillgruber). At first sight this sounds convincing; yet contrary evidence exists in Hitler's own words. To Walter Hewel, a man and confidant within his closest circle (Hewel killed himself the day after Hitler's suicide in 1945), he said on 29 May: once Russia is defeated, "this will force England to make peace. Hope this year." He spoke to General Franz Halder, who wrote it in his war diary on 14 June: Hitler calculates "that the collapse of Russia will induce England to give up the struggle. The main enemy is still Britain."* On 21 June he talked again with Hewel at some length, who jotted down: "The Führer expects a lot from the Russian campaign. . . . He thinks that England will have to give in." Then he dictated his long letter to Mussolini, replete with his global speculations, emphasizing over and over again that England was on the verge of defeat. "The situation in England itself is bad. . . . [They have only] hopes. These hopes are based solely on the assumption: Russia and America. We have no chance of eliminating America. But it does lie in our power to eliminate Russia."†

What Hitler did not tell Mussolini (or Goebbels) was another, very important, decision he made on that fateful day. He issued a peremptory order to every German naval vessel and submarine craft in the Atlantic. Avoid, *under all circumstances* (he underlined this) firing at American vessels; do not

* Halder, *Kriegstagebuch.* See also Goebbels, *Tagebücher,* 18 June, about Churchill: "Were it not for him, this war would have ended long ago."
† *NSR,* 351.

even return fire when attacked by Americans. He wanted to avoid any incident or pretext that could make it easier for Roosevelt to declare war on Germany.* He hoped against hope that — unlikely but perhaps — the United States could be kept out of a real war against him. But if Russia is eliminated . . . Then it may become impossible for Roosevelt and Churchill to continue their war against him.

We may have to correct, or at least question, yet another widely accepted view of Hitler: that, consumed by megalomania — or call it hubris, or call it overconfidence — he had no doubts about the power of his armies to crush Russia. All through June the German generals, without exception, were sure of their capacity to smash the Russian armed forces. Yet on 21 June, Himmler told Heydrich: "the Führer is not so optimistic as his military advisers." Either that day or the day before, someone spoke of Russia as "a big bubble." Hitler suddenly became thoughtful. He said that Russia was rather like a ship in *The Flying Dutchman*. He added: "The beginning of every war is like opening the door into a dark room. One never knows what is hidden in the darkness."† On

---

* He did not revoke that order until 8 December, hours after Pearl Harbor and three days before his declaration of war against the United States.

† Lukacs, *Last European War,* 139. Zoller, *Hitler Privat,* 142–143, remarks of one of Hitler's secretaries, Frau Christa Schroeder. Forty years later Schroeder's own reminiscences, *Er war mein Chef,* 113: "Russia was always uncanny [unheimlich] for him, something like the ghost ship in *The Flying Dutchman*. To my question of why he keeps repeating that this decision [going against Russia] is his most difficult one, he answered:

21 June his adjutant Nicolaus Below noted that Hitler was "increasingly nervous and restless. He talked a lot, walked up and down, he seemed impatient, waiting for something." In the early afternoon he decided to go out for a brief automobile ride, which was not his custom. The last friend he saw that day was Goebbels. He liked Goebbels, even though he seldom discussed serious military matters with him. During the previous two days they had, among other things, talked about and listened to different orchestrations of fanfares, a harmonization of trumpet sounds announcing extraordinary military news on the Greater German Reich radio network. They then discussed at what hour Hitler's proclamation announcing the new war should be broadcast. Goebbels and his friends had just finished watching (for the second time) the American film *Gone with the Wind,* which Goebbels much admired. After that came Hitler's telephone call for Goebbels to come over to the Chancellery. They talked, walking up and down in Hitler's drawing room for a long time. They agreed that Hitler's proclamation would be read on the Greater German radio at 5:30 next morning. Goebbels left Hitler at half past two.* This was not unusual for Hitler, whose habit was to go to bed late at night and rise late in the morning.

---

because Russia may be a big soap bubble but it also could be something quite different."

*Before going to bed Hitler said to his adjutant: "This will be the hardest struggle that our soldiers have to bear in this war." Below, *Als Hitlers Adjutant,* 279.

CHAPTER FIVE

MOSCOW

On the morning of 22 June, Hitler had his customary amount of sleep. Stalin had not. He retired after the men of the Politburo had left: according to Mikoyan, this was close to three, according to Molotov at one. Around four the telephone rang. It was Zhukov. The first German bombs had already been cast on Russian cities and towns; German troops, guns, horses, and tanks were already well within Soviet territory. For a few minutes Stalin was not roused. According to Zhukov, he did not speak at first, and his breathing was heavy. Then he got up and dressed and told the Politburo to come to his office in the Kremlin at once. They arrived around half past four. Most of them remember that Stalin was subdued and pale. At least according to Mikoyan he still murmured once that "this might be a provocation by German officers."

One hour before that Ribbentrop's telegram arrived in the German embassy, with the declaration of war (even though Hitler avoided that term), instructing Schulenburg to communicate it to Molotov at once. It took not more than three or four minutes for Molotov to walk upstairs from Stalin's office to his own. We have a fairly authentic account of this, the last and dramatic meeting between Molotov and Schulenburg, mostly from the memoirs of Gustav Hilger, Schulenburg's counselor, who was present. The rigid, slab-faced Molotov was, for once, "visibly struggling with deep inner excitement. . . . He wore a tired and worn-out expression." Schulenburg read the text of the note. Molotov asked: "Is this supposed to be a declaration of war?" "Schulenburg reacted in silence with a gesture characteristic of him; he drew up his shoulders and turned up his hands." Molotov spoke. "*Without any reason* [he emphasized this] Germany had attacked a country with which it had concluded a pact of non-aggression and friendship. . . . Surely we have not deserved this."* Molotov's language is telling. (It was not different from Dekanozov's in Berlin: "Wasn't there a mistake?" The official Soviet version does not include that Molotovian sentence.) His recollections of that night are con-

---

* Hilger, *Incompatible Allies,* 336 (I have made a slight change in the inadequate English translation of Hilger's description of Schulenburg's gesture.)

fusing and often erroneous. Undoubtedly, he was following Stalin's instructions.*

When he came downstairs, Stalin asked: "Well, is this a declaration of war?" Molotov nodded.

The others now suggested that Stalin speak to the people of the Russias. He refused: no, he said, let Molotov do that, later in the day.

The people of Moscow woke on a very hot Sunday morning, knowing nothing about the war. There was nothing in the newspapers, nor on the radio. Moscow radio began its usual Sunday program of calisthenics, broadcasting other routine items of news. The few men and women who learned something got it from foreign broadcasts. When the chief of foreign intelligence of the NKVD, Fitin, was driven back to Moscow from his dacha, he saw groups of high school students marching and singing, celebrating their graduation. When he arrived in his office, he was told the news of the war. During the last days he had sent more than one intelligence report to the Kremlin. He must have been one of the few

---

* Chou En-Lai (much later the foreign minister and chief statesman of Communist China, but then in Chungking, close to Chiang Kai-Shek) telegraphed to Dimitrov on 21 June that Germany would start the war within twenty-four hours. Dimitrov rang up Molotov (who had no wish to see him) about this. Molotov said nothing, except, "The situation is unclear. A great game is being played. Not everything depends on us." There is a (somewhat unclear) suggestion in the Goebbels diaries that as a last attempt Molotov had hoped to be allowed to come to Berlin around 15 June.

people in Moscow who were relieved: had his earlier warnings proved untrue, he could have been demoted, imprisoned, or even executed.

One other person relieved was the anonymous Russian who dialed the telephone number of the British embassy. He said that he wanted to speak to an Englishman. The Russian porter downstairs called a minor staff member to the switchboard. On that empty Sunday Harold Elvin was in charge of the building. He heard a Russian say: "We fight together I think?" "Yes, I think so," the Englishman said. "I shake your hand." "Thank you. Good wishes." Later that morning Elvin walked to Red Square and sat in a café. "The populace moved as heretofore. I bored the faces for some change of expression or emotion. Nothing, absolutely nothing." That was an hour after Molotov's broadcast announcing the war. Another Englishman saw that hardly anyone stopped when the megaphones bellowed out Molotov's speech; wherever they were going they walked on.* The British chargé d'affaires, Baggalay, called at the Foreign Ministry. He was received by Vishinsky. They listened to Molotov's speech together.

Molotov's wooden tones (and, on one occasion, his stammering) were not very impressive, but that did not matter; Stalin said that it was all right, nothing else. It may be interesting that Stalin spent more time with Beria than with Zhukov on that day; however, in the early afternoon he issued the order of general mobilization. It seems that he was

---

* Elvin, *Cockney in Moscow*, 58–59.

worried about the mind of the population: besides his secret police satrap Beria he gave orders to A. S. Shcherbakov, the party (and police) chief in Moscow, to secure the city and flood it with his agents; among other measures all Germans in Moscow were to be arrested immediately. All those who saw or spoke with Stalin on 22 June found him worn and tired.* He left his office early, before five, driven to Kuntsevo for a badly needed sleep, no doubt. He came back to work in his Kremlin office after three in the morning next day.

* According to Dimitrov's diary he said that day: "They attacked us, without having asked anything from us, without requesting any kind of negotiations." That is: why had not Hitler demanded something from him, no matter what? . . . Were these still Stalin's inclinations? Likely so — except that Dimitrov did not see him on 22 June. (Did he say this on the telephone? Did he at all find time to talk to Dimitrov that day?)

CHAPTER SIX

London

In London, too, the 22nd of June was a day of hot sunshine, sinking into a warm evening. The Sunday newspapers had been printed before the invasion. The British people heard the news of the new war from the BBC; and then their prime minister spoke to them at nine that night.

How different was London from Moscow and even from Berlin then! We may as well contemplate a vanished world. There were still roses in the parks and squares; women in printed frocks and wide-brimmed straw hats walking into churches; shiny automobiles moving around Mayfair; a few well-booted horsemen and -women still seen trotting or cantering in Richmond Park; the London Underground rumbling beneath the stony thoroughfares. Hundreds of buildings had burned out or been destroyed by bombs in the City and in the East End, more than in Berlin. But the mental climate was that of a summer Sunday, quietude without commotion.

The people of Britain were prepared for the sudden news of the German invasion of Russia. There was their element of relief: suddenly another war begun by Hitler; so Britain was not again alone. George Orwell wrote in his diary: "Talking to people in the Home Guard, including Blimps and quite wealthy business men, I find everyone completely pro-Russian, though much divided about the Russian capacity to resist. . . . All spoken in ignorance, but showing what people's sentiments are."*

There were people close to the captain and to the high bridge of the ship of state who, while they knew that a great turning point in the relations of the Third Reich and the Soviet Union was coming close, thought that Stalin would make another deal with Hitler instead of war. They included John Winant, the American ambassador to Britain, and — at least to some extent — Sir Stafford Cripps who had flown home from Moscow, dejected by his treatment there. But by

---

* Orwell, *Collected Essays*, 2:403. (There was a precedent to this: in 1914 a rumor swept the British isles that Russian troops had landed in Scotland on their way to the western front in France they were seen with snow on their boots.) Also, Orwell's diary for 27 June: "Everyone is remarking in anticipation what a bore the Free Russians will be. It is forecast that they will be just like the White Russians. People have visions of Stalin in a little shop in Putney, selling samovars and doing Caucasian dances etc etc."

about 15 June informed people tended to believe that Hitler would attack, and soon. Churchill had no doubts about that. Intelligence and other information about the German invasion of Russia were now coagulating into a mass.* Not that Churchill was particularly cheerful. "Battleaxe," the first British offensive against General Rommel in North Africa, began on 15 June; after two days it became obvious that it had failed. For a while Churchill walked up and down disconsolately in the gardens at Chequers. But he slept well and returned to work energetic and confident. Still, he had yet other anxieties with which to deal. He knew that in the United States, isolationist sentiments, including anti-Communism, were rife. They might flare up if and when Russia came into the war. He drafted a letter to Roosevelt about that.

He went to the small cottage at Chartwell, his country house in Kent. For several days there was unbroken sunshine, a warm haze, a massing riot of flowers. On Friday the 20th he went down to Dover to see one of his pet projects, a huge gun occasionally firing giant shells across the Channel. On Saturday he lunched at 10 Downing Street and went back to Chequers. During dinner he said, "A German attack on Russia is certain and Russia will be defeated."† In any event, he said

*At this time intelligence had begun to include decrypts from the German secret military code machines ("Enigma," later to be code-named "Ultra").

† Colville, *Fringes of Power,* 404.

that he would go "all out" to help Russia and thought that the United States would do the same. Hitler, he thought, was foolish to depend on anti-Communist sympathies among the English-speaking peoples. After dinner he walked in the garden with his secretary Jock Colville. There he uttered a since celebrated phrase. Colville had asked whether his uncompromising idea of helping the Soviet Union did not mean that he, Churchill, was now denying his old and principled anti-Communist beliefs. Churchill said no. "If Hitler invaded Hell [he] would make at least a favorable reference to the Devil!"* (One of the many examples when Churchill's pleasure in his instant powers of half-serious wit would mark — rather than mar — his record.)

At four at dawn on Sunday, 22 June, the first news of the German invasion arrived. Churchill's orders were never to waken him except in the event of a German invasion of England. At seven Colville went around Chequers with the news to the other guests. When Churchill awoke a few minutes before eight, he told Colville to call the BBC: he will broadcast to the nation (and to the world) that night.

It may be of some interest to follow Churchill during that sunny day — more precisely: to witness some of the expressions of his mind. Often he has been described as a great war leader but also as a supreme opportunist and therefore — to some people — shortsighted, dominated as he was by his ob-

---

* Hitler to his Gauleiters, explaining himself on 28 August 1939: "A Pact with a Satan, in order to drive the Devil out." Below, *Als Hitlers Adjutant,* 183.

session to destroy Hitler and crush Germany. This is not the place to discuss these great issues, but I may as well assert that about the essential matter of Russia, Churchill was startlingly consistent. In 1940, as well as in 1941 and later, he saw the alternatives clearly and simply: either all of Europe would be ruled by Germany (for a long time), or the eastern half of Europe would be ruled for Russia (probably not for long), and half of Europe was better than none. Contrary to his many critics, contrary to many Germans, he was not blinded or duped by Stalin, notwithstanding his occasionally florid tributes to the latter during the war. On that fateful June Sunday he said what he knew: the great issue was not Communism, it was Russia. Tonight he would say this to the British people and to the world. He took his usual hot bath, looked in his red box at the latest items, came down to breakfast, and sat down at eleven to write his speech. He worked on it during the entire day, finishing it but a few minutes before nine, after the microphones were already set up.

Meanwhile his guests came down from their flowers-and-chintz rooms in Chequers or drove up the graveled driveway, on occasion interrupting his work, which he customarily did not mind. There were his Foreign Secretary Eden, the American ambassador, Lord Beaverbrook, Viscount Cranborne, Sir John Dill, then chief of the Imperial General Staff, Sir Stafford and Lady Cripps; the prime minister of New Zealand (Peter Fraser) came later. Eden was driven off early to the Foreign Office in London, which of course became busy that day. Among other matters he called for the Russian ambassador to come at noon.* Ambassador John Winant was the only one who still thought that Stalin might yet come to a deal with Hitler. At lunch Churchill dominated the conversation, taunting Cripps, telling him that Communists and Communism were among the lowest sort of humankind. At dinner, which began late, after Churchill's broadcast, the arguments continued, to his considerable pleasure. He said that he had decided that there ought not be a debate in Parliament about the issue of aid to Russia. Colville watched the discussion back and forth. "The P.M.'s view was that Russia was now at war; innocent peasants were being slaughtered; and we should forget about Soviet systems or the Comintern and extend our hand to fellow human beings in distress. The argument was extremely vehement. I have never spent a more enjoyable evening."†

"No one has been a more consistent opponent of Communism than I have for the last twenty-five years, I will unsay no word that I have spoken about it. But all this fades away before the spectacle now unfolding. . . . I see the Russian sol-

* Ivan M. Maisky, as usual, had spent the weekend in Bovingdon, in the country house of Juan Negrín, the exiled "head" of the former Red government in Spain. On Saturday he had an urgent telephone call from Cripps; he drove back to his embassy, where Cripps told him that according to the latest and reliable information, the German invasion would begin next day at dawn, or, perhaps, on the 29th. At eight on Sunday morning (it was already afternoon in Moscow) his embassy people called him at Negrín's to tell him that the war had begun. He went back to London to hear Molotov's speech. That night he would hear Churchill's. But for the next four or five days he was told nothing from Moscow.

† Colville, *Fringes of Power,* 405–406.

diers standing on the threshold of their native land, guarding the fields which their fathers have tilled from time immemorial. I see them guarding their homes where mothers and wives pray—ah yes, for there are times when all pray—for the safety of their loved ones, the return of the bread-winner, of their champion, of their protector. . . . I have to declare the decision of His Majesty's Government . . . for we must speak out now at once, without a day's delay. I have to make the declaration, but can you doubt what our policy will be? We have but one aim and one single, irrevocable purpose. We are resolved to destroy Hitler and every vestige of the Nazi regime. From this nothing will turn us—nothing. . . . Any man or state who fights on against Nazidom will have our aid. . . . It follows, therefore, that we shall give whatever help we can to Russia and the Russian people." Thus Churchill spoke to the world when night fell in London on 22 June.*

* Churchill, *Grand Alliance,* 371–373. Like most of his speeches, the effect is even stronger when read than when heard. The opposite applies to Hitler's.

CHAPTER SEVEN

Washington — and Across the World

Across Eurasia broke the news on 22 June. To the United States it came the night before, sometime before midnight in the East, earlier in the Midwest and the West. But most of the Sunday newspapers had been printed; there was no chance to change their early editions except here and there. The readers and the commentators of the great radio networks broadcast the news, including American newsmen in London and even in Berlin. President Roosevelt was prepared for it. On Saturday, 21 June, he had a fairly leisurely day. The Crown Princess Martha of Norway, a beautiful woman of whom he was very fond, came to the White House that afternoon; they were talking together for more than two hours. Then there was an unusually long dinner (neither dinners nor their menus were long during the Roosevelts' tenure), including the crown princess, Roosevelt's son Elliott, and other guests, a few of them staying for the night. We have no record of their conversation, which surely must have included something about Russia. During the dinner, a little before ten, there was a shock. The president's favorite secretary, Missy Le Hand, became suddenly ill; she left the dinner table and was then sped to Doctors' Hospital. The other guests left about half an hour later. It seems that Hitler's proclamation of war did not reach the president until next morning, since the time of its broadcast in Berlin would have been nearly midnight in Washington, where Roosevelt (unlike Hitler and Stalin and Churchill) had the habit of going to bed early.

A week before, Churchill had sent him a letter. One of its five paragraphs (and the longest) dealt with Russia. "From every source at my disposal including some most trustworthy it looks as if a vast German onslaught on the Russian frontier is imminent. . . . Should this new war break out we shall of course give all encouragement and any help we can spare to the Russians, following the principle that Hitler is the foe we have to beat. I do not expect any class political reactions here and trust that a German-Russian conflict will not cause you any embarrassment."

Churchill knew what he was writing about. There was no division in Roosevelt's mind; there were no divided counsels around him; but there was a division among the American people. Save for an influential minority, they did not want their country to be involved in a European war, even though the majority of Americans disliked Hitler. Another minority were called "isolationists," an imprecise word. In 1941 and before isolationists included not only nationalists but also pacifists and even some American socialists. But American isolationism has never been consistent: most of the committed isolationists who were openly opposed to American intervention against Hitler's Germany five years later became the vocal supporters of an aggressive American intervention against the Soviet Union. The main characteristic of the "isolationists" in 1939 and 1940 was their distrust of Britain and France; in June 1941 and immediately thereafter it was their hatred of the Soviet Union. Many (though not all) of them were Republicans; as elsewhere in the world, too, anti-Communism in the United States was a powerful inclination. There were innumerable examples of this. On 23 June the America First committee declared, "The entry of Communist Russia into the war certainly should settle once and for all the intervention issue here at home. The war party can hardly ask the people of America to take up arms behind the red flag." A few days later the former president Herbert Hoover said: "Now we find ourselves promising aid to Stalin and his militant conspiracy against the whole democratic ideals of the world. . . . If we go further and join the war and we win then we have won for Stalin; the grip of

Communism on Russia, and more opportunity for it to extend in the world."* In sum, Communism was worse; more, it was more dangerous than National Socialism. (Senator Robert A. Taft said this a few days before Pearl Harbor, when the Germans stood fifteen miles before Moscow.) That was not quite in accord with what American public opinion, its representatives and propagators thought and said on 22 June and after; but it was a factor that Roosevelt had to consider.

He was cautious, as almost always. Unlike Churchill, he made no statement on 22 June or for many days afterward. (A statement of his Undersecretary of State Sumner Welles was largely in accord with Churchill's words.) Hitler (who has been almost always described as ignorant about America and Americans) knew that—whence his order not to fire back at Americans, even in extreme circumstances at sea. He hoped, too, that his war against Communist Russia might turn to his advantage. There were some instances of this after 22 June, but not enough. A few, but only a few, Catholic bishops and publications across the world did welcome the German "crusade." On 23 June a Spanish mob, arranged by Franco's government, demonstrated and attempted to attack the British embassy in Madrid, shouting "Gibraltar!" Soon Franco would furnish and send a volunteer division to Hitler. But Pope Pius XII, fearful of Communism ever since his experiences in Munich in 1919, remained silent, as did the

---

* *Time,* 7 July 1941. *Catholic World,* August 1941: "To defend democracy with the help of Stalin would be like calling on Jesse James or John Dillinger to maintain law and order."

entire diplomatic and bureaucratic staff of the Vatican. The twenty-second of June was an empty Sunday in Rome. Mussolini had gone to the seashore to bathe and swim in the sea.

Throughout German-occupied Europe men and women rejoiced in the news. Perhaps Hitler would get into real trouble now, they thought and said. Similar, though not unequivocal, sentiments were current among the Polish people, despite their ancient and modern fears and hatreds of Russia and Russians. Gladdened were the threatened and tortured Jews across Europe, still not knowing what their awful fate would be soon. On the other side Finns and Rumanians, who had been attacked by Russia only a year before, welcomed the German invasion. Behind the retreating Russians, listening to the rolling thunder of German armor, guns, and airplanes, many Lithuanians, Letts, Estonians, Ukrainians were ready to acclaim the Germans as their liberators. But here we are running ahead of our story.

There is no need to spend more than a few short sentences on Communists across the world on that day. They had accepted — true, many of them with a sour taste in their mouths and stomachs — Stalin's pact with Hitler in 1939. On 22 June they were, too, instantly relieved of their agonies — if agonies those had been at all. Stalin was now their savior, if not The Savior of Mankind.

PART III

Unintended Consequences

CHAPTER EIGHT

The Immediate Crisis

I

On the twenty-second of June — as indeed during weeks before as well as after that fateful day — the best military experts throughout the world predicted the defeat of the Soviet Union within a few weeks, or within two months at the most. These estimates were about the same on both sides of the world struggle. Four to six weeks, generals and heads of intelligence services predicted; six or eight weeks, estimated others; that is what it would take for the armies of the Third Reich to destroy the armed forces of the Soviet Union, to conquer European Russia. These predictions were not unreasonable. They rested on evidence of the Russian army's lamentable performance against the Finns during the Winter War; on the no less considerable evidence of the mutilation and the disarray of the upper ranks of the Russian military due to Stalin's purges; on the circumstantial but telling evidence of how Stalin and Molotov and presumably other Russian leaders tried their best or, rather, worst to please Hitler and to avoid war thus; and — last but not least — on their more than considerable respect for the capacity and ability of the German armies in this war. Oddly — or perhaps not so oddly — such were the opinions of men who were stationed in Moscow and who knew Soviet conditions fairly well. So, for example, held the American ambassador to Moscow, Laurence Steinhardt — whereas his shallow and often foolish predecessor Joseph Davies tried (and successfully) to convince Franklin Roosevelt that Russia would hold out and sooner rather than later win. As late as mid-August another former American ambassador to Moscow, the intelligent and perceptive William C. Bullitt, spoke in Philadelphia to the American Legion: "I know no man in Washington who believes that the Soviet army can defeat the German army." On 23 June the secretary of war, Henry Stimson, reported the consensus of the American Chiefs of Staff to Roosevelt: "Germany will be thoroughly occupied in beating Russia for a minimum of one month and a possible maximum of three months."

And that was, by and large, what Churchill expected, too: at best, a large breath of temporary relief for Britain. He did not begin to change his mind about Russia's prospects until about late October. His great adversary Hitler allowed himself to be carried away by the unexpectedly rapid advance of his armies during the first week of the war. On 28 June he dropped a remark to one of his secretaries, Frau Schroeder: "In four weeks we are in Moscow. Moscow will be razed to the ground."

This book is not a military history of the German-Russian war, and not even of its first months. However, I must sum up something about the immediate impact of that 22nd of June. The German army pouring into the Russias amounted to more than three million men, more than three thousand armored vehicles, six hundred thousand motors, more than ten thousand horses, more than seven thousand guns; above them flew and behind them were readied more than two thousand airplanes. These are formidable numbers, though necessarily not accurate ones, since not all of these men and things were instantly on the move; on the other hand, they were being replenished from day to day. More telling for our purposes was the unpreparedness of the Russians at the very beginning. Stalin was of course largely responsible for that; but consider, too, that his reluctance to fully prepare for war had something to do with his own knowledge of the incomplete organization of the Soviet army. That should not relieve him of his responsibility. His directives against responding to German airplanes flying photographic missions over the western Soviet Union alone allowed Göring's Luftwaffe to destroy more than 1,200 Russian aircraft on their airfields on the first day of the war. On the ground, too, the

Germans' spearheads were racing ahead, at times without any effective opposition from masses of Russian troops, who were not only unprepared but surprised by the suddenness of this war. One exception was the courageous Russian defense of the old citadel of Brest, around which German motorized troops rumbled forward. Russian unpreparedness and weak resistance were especially apparent at the center of the front, involving the Russian Fourth Army. This was nothing like the traditional Russian practice of a cautious, calculated, cunning retreat. Instead there were signs of panic, and a — for a time increasing — lack of communications, with the result that the Germans reached and broke into Minsk, nearly two hundred miles from their starting points at the border, after six days of desultory fighting.

We have seen that on 22 June, Stalin had refused to address the peoples of the Soviet Union. According to Mikoyan, he said: "What can I tell the people?" During the next few days he saw Molotov much more often than he saw anyone else. He did order calling up all men between twenty-two and thirty-six. On the 23rd he decided to form the Stavka (another word from tsarist times), the General Supreme Command consisting of three generals, one admiral, Molotov, Voroshilov, and himself as chairman and supreme commander. His (and its) first instructions were verbose and often unreasonable, if not senseless; but then reports from the front were confused and confusing. It may be significant that he devoted extraordinary attention to the departure of the German embassy, with Schulenburg at its head. On Monday, 23 June, he instructed his own interpreter and appointed a special officer in charge to call on Schulenburg and ascertain whether the ambassador had any particular requests. When two weeks later Schulenburg, on his way home to Germany via Turkey, met Franz von Papen, the German ambassador there, he said that he thought that even then Stalin might still have hoped for "some kind of a tacit agreement with Hitler." It did not come to that. But the hope to halt the war somehow was still current in Stalin's mind and in the minds of some of the Politburo men, especially as the German thrust into the bowels of the Soviet Union progressed incredibly fast and seemed perhaps irreversible.

Here we come to a significant episode. Often it is the head of the secret police who knows more about the deadly dangers confronting the state than does almost anybody else; and so he is inclined to act on his own. That is how Joseph Fouché in France acted in 1814; that is what Himmler attempted on a few occasions in 1944 and 1945, with or without Hitler's assent. Notwithstanding Stalin's inclinations and directives, by early June, Beria convinced himself that the German invasion was coming.* There is telling (but also to some extent disputable) evidence that five days after the German invasion Beria made a move to inquire about some

---

* Consider that Beria's feelings about Stalin were not simple: they were a compound of obedience and fear, of respect and hate, as indeed appeared in his words and behavior at the time of Stalin's death in 1953.

kind of a Russian surrender in exchange for Hitler's halting the war. He ordered one of his men, swearing absolute secrecy, to try to establish some contact with Berlin. The middleman was to be Ivan Todorov Stamenov, the Bulgarian minister in Moscow. (Bulgaria was the only state bound to Germany with a pact that did not declare war on Russia; Hitler, aware of Bulgaria's ancient ties with Russia, had not required that; and in accord with international diplomatic practice, Bulgaria was to represent the remnant German interests in Moscow after the break of German-Russian relations.) It seems that Beria instructed his agent (Pavel Sudoplatov) in person, walking up and down the street before his apartment house. Sudoplatov would meet Stamenov at a table in Beria's favorite restaurant and propose the surrender of the Baltic states and of the Ukraine if Germany would halt the further advance of its armies. The meeting then took place over a midday meal: but Stamenov allegedly told Sudoplatov that there was no sense for him to report this to Sofia and consequently to Berlin, because the Germans would get lost in Russia even if they were to drive the Russian armies as far back as the Urals. It seems that Beria (and probably others, too) was thinking of a desperate move to repeat Brest-Litovsk, where in early 1918 Lenin agreed to a large-scale German occupation of the western portions of the former Russian empire in order to save his Bolshevik rule in the rest. We cannot ascertain whether Stalin (and Molotov) knew about Beria's attempt to recruit Stamenov. Yet it must not be doubted that the potential consideration of a Brest-Litovsk existed also in their minds.*

2

"Nemesis," Churchill wrote, personifies the Goddess of Retribution. "War is mainly a catalogue of blunders, but it may be doubted whether any mistake in history has equalled that of which Stalin and the Communist chiefs were guilty when

---

*The documentary evidence of this episode is there in a long memorandum written by Sudoplatov in August 1953—after Stalin's death, and after Beria had been arrested by Khrushchev and Co., Stalin's successors. This document has been printed in *1941 g.*, doc. 651, but with the endnote that in other Russian archives, papers or documents of such a meeting between Sudoplatov and Stamenov were not found. Still, there is some indirect evidence involving Stamenov himself, who seems to have been allowed to live comfortably under the Bulgarian Communist regime (he died in 1959). Allegedly in 1953 two men were sent to Sofia from Moscow to interrogate Stamenov, who did not tell them anything. We also ought to consider Sudoplatov's purposes in writing this memorandum in July or August 1953. He had every reason to save his skin, to disassociate himself from Beria, indeed, to accuse Beria of "treason" (these are his words at the end of the memorandum) at a time when Beria's closest henchmen (Dekanozov, for example) were about to share Beria's fate, execution. According to Sudoplatov, Beria acted without letting anyone else in the Soviet government know. According to Volkogonov, Stalin and Molotov knew—indeed, he reports that they met with Stamenov, which I consider wholly implausible. Recent writings about this episode may be found in Pleshakov, *Stalin's Folly* (which is inaccurate throughout), and in articles by Chizhikov and Nabojshchikov.

they . . . supinely awaited, or were incapable of realising the fearful onslaught which impended upon Russia. . . . The force, the mass, the bravery and endurance of Mother Russia had still to be thrown into the scale. But so far as strategy, policy, foresight, competence are arbiters, Stalin and his commissars showed themselves at this moment the most completely outwitted bunglers of the Second World War."* Sixty-five years after 1941, and more than fifty-five years after Churchill wrote these sentences, his words sound proper and right. And yet we may question whether all would have turned out in the end differently had Stalin and the Russian armed force been ready to fight the Germans in June 1941 or even earlier. Perhaps "the force of Mother Russia" would have been thrown into the scale too early? We cannot tell.

What we can tell is that Stalin, whose mental powers were indeed considerable, was (unlike Churchill or Hitler) a man of slow reactions. (We know that after the suicide of his wife in 1932 it took a week or so before he suffered something like a mental collapse.) In 1941 the full impact of impending defeat and potential collapse struck him not on 22 June but on the following Saturday, the 28th, when he learned that Germans were in Minsk and when communications with the central front had become temporarily unmanageable, here and there broken down. That night, in his Kremlin office, there was a furious exchange between him and Generals Zhukov and Timoshenko. Both Mikoyan and Molotov, very

---

* Churchill, *Grand Alliance,* 352–353.

different men, recalled that Stalin was suddenly very depressed. About ten he chose to stomp out of his office, ordering some of his minions to accompany him to Kuntsevo. On the steps going down his voice rose. "Everything is lost. I give up. What Lenin had founded we f——d up." He repeated this once more. "We f——d or sh——d it all up."* We need not parse these ugly words, the outbursts of this peasant tsar.

Molotov, Mikoyan, Malenkov, and Co. thought for a while that their leader spoke thus also because he wanted to frighten them, for effect. Yet this was not quite so. For the next two days Stalin closeted himself in his Kuntsevo dacha, closing out the world. He did not return to his Kremlin office the next day or the day after. More ominously, he could not be reached in his dacha. Once or twice his secretary answered the telephone calls in a wooden tone, saying that he did not know and could not tell where Stalin was. Two days and two nights passed. Late in the evening of Monday, 30 June, the men of the Politburo decided, nervously, to drive out to the dacha, whether they were invited or not. They found Stalin haggard. His first words were: "Why did

---

* Montefiore, *Stalin,* 373 et seq. Stalin's invocation of Lenin is interesting. Did it suggest his respectful admiration for Lenin, who had established the Soviet state? Probably — but is it not possible that he was thinking also of the Lenin who established that state but who was also willing to pay the (temporary) price at Brest-Litovsk to the Germans to save what was possible? If so, Stalin on the night of 28 June must have known that a new Brest-Litovsk was no longer possible — not with the German armies racing ahead, not with Hitler.

you come?" He thought—or at least it seemed—that they had come to depose and arrest him. No: they were more frightened than he was. There was a short and desultory exchange of phrases. At least two of them asked him "to come back to work." Stalin turned to them and asked or, rather, thought out loud: Yes, but "Can I live up to people's hopes any longer? Can I lead the country to final victory? There may be more deserving candidates." No, they said— you must lead.

Then he recovered from his collapse. Next morning he came back to his Kremlin office. He began to reorganize posts of command, military and civilian. He began to plan his speech to the nation. That he gave two days later, on 3 July. He did not use the customary Communist words and phrases. His speech, even though delivered in a low voice, had immediate effects: Russians and other peoples of the Soviet Union responded to what seemed a patriotic call, issued by their leader, his first clear and strong encouragement since the war had started, more than ten days before. They knew nothing of their leader's collapse of will. That immediate crisis was now over, while the breakup of the Russian armies along the broken fronts went on.

Let us pause for a moment. Exactly thirteen months before that twenty-eighth of June in Moscow, on the twenty-eighth of May in London, Winston Churchill made—or, more precisely, carried through—his great historic decision. Like Stalin and Russia in 1941, he and his England in May 1940 were facing disaster after disaster. Their only army was encircled in Dunkirk. But Churchill said to his cabinet: "Of course, whatever happens at Dunkirk, we will fight on." Unlike Russia in 1941, England in 1940 could have received an offer of peace from Hitler. He would not demolish the British Empire. What he wanted from Britain was to accept his complete domination of Europe and to cease resisting Germany. Churchill would not consider that for a moment; he knew that this would mean England becoming a junior partner of Germany, if not "a slave state." In 1940 Churchill stood up to Hitler; he was the man who was the single obstacle to Hitler's winning the Second World War. In 1941 Stalin was not alone, he was about to become the partner of Churchill and Roosevelt. Yet if Hitler would only have halted his armies in 1941 Stalin might have been willing to become his junior partner, indeed, to turn over to Hitler portions of his empire if need be, while the rest of Europe could go to hell. Hitler knew that. But he thought that his armies could conquer Russia. In 1940 he was not sure that he could conquer England. It was then Churchill, not Stalin, who was the obstacle to his complete triumph. Because of this he hated Churchill and then turned to hate the English people with a fury, till the end. He did not hate Stalin; once his invasion of Russia bogged down, he respected him, he even said that he liked him. Such is the irony of history — or, rather, the alchemy of the human mind.

CHAPTER NINE

Unintended Consequences

I

About twenty-four hours before Stalin's historic address something happened in Tokyo that was — almost — as decisive, as consequential as was Hitler's invasion of the Soviet Union on 22 June. A secret conference (a crown council) met in the palace of the Emperor Hirohito. The conclave lasted, according to one source, nearly sixteen hours. Imperial Japan had a choice. Her opportunity, as in the First World War, was to advance in the Far East while the great European powers were tearing at each other on the other side of the globe. Yet unlike during the First World War, this was now complicated by an increasing conflict between

Japan and the United States in the Pacific. Despite all of their previous information about the imminent German-Russian war, the Japanese government paid less attention to that than to the problem of their relations with the United States. But now there was a change. Their foreign minister Matsuoka argued that Japan should instantly attack the Soviet Union and invade the Russian Far East as the Germans attacked European Russia. He went so far as to request a special audience with the emperor even before the crown council meeting; he wished to promote his proposition of a Japanese war against the Soviet Union. This from a man who had signed the nonaggression pact with Stalin less than three months before, who had drunk copiously to their mutual health in a jolly ceremony in the Kremlin, and who often spoke about the supposedly unique virtue of "bushido," meaning Japanese chivalry. No matter: on that second of July in 1941, Matsuoka lost. The conferees discussed the three alternatives before Japan: (1) move southward and prepare for a war with Britain and the United States; (2) move westward and attack the Soviet Union forthwith; (3) do not yet move eastward, mitigating the prospect of such a war through negotiations with the United States. They eschewed (2) and chose (1), partially and temporarily mitigated by (3). That eventually led to Pearl Harbor and thereafter to the destruction of the Japanese empire. It was the worst of decisions. It allowed, among other things, Roosevelt to enter the war finally not only against Japan but also against Germany. That happened in December 1941, at the very moment when half a globe away the Russians before Moscow turned the Germans back for the first time.

It is impossible to calculate what would have happened if the Japanese had attacked the Soviet Union in the east, forcing Stalin to fight a two-front war. What we know is the existence of information that Stalin would now take seriously. The prime agent of the Russians in Tokyo, Richard Sorge, performed a service to Moscow even greater than with his disregarded precise warnings during the weeks before 22 June. Sorge was found out and arrested in Tokyo in October, but the result was the transfer and transport of considerable Russian troops from the Far Eastern frontier region to the European-Russian front. Historians and other writers have since taken for granted that this mass transfer was the decisive factor that saved Moscow in December 1941. It was an important element in the military balance, whether it gave *the* decisive tilt in the struggle at the central front or not. In any event, all three statesmen, Stalin, Churchill, and Roosevelt, profited from the Japanese decision to move south, not west. We have seen that in June 1941 Roosevelt, unlike Churchill, said little or nothing in public of his decision to stand by and support Russia, because he knew that he had both actual and potential opposition to such a declaration within the United States, an opposition that then became suddenly silent, after Pearl Harbor melting — temporarily — away. In any event, the Japanese decision not to attack the Soviet Union saved Roosevelt from a dilemma. Had Japan attacked Russia in the Far East, there is every reason to believe that Roosevelt would have made certain threatening moves against the Japanese in the northern Pacific; yet it is doubtful that a Japanese attack against Russia would have been sufficient for Roosevelt to ask for a declaration of war. At Yalta in 1945 he and Stalin divided much of the Far East between themselves.* Then came the total defeat of Japan. Yet a few years after that it appeared that the ultimate profiteer of the Second World War (and of the subsequent Korean War) in the Far East was not the United States, and surely not Russia, but China — unintended consequences, indeed.

2

The sentiment and ideology of anti-Communism were Roosevelt's problem within the United States. Hitler knew that. He also hoped that anti-Communism, which had made it easy for him to recruit support both within Germany and beyond it, would help garner allies for his war against the Soviet Union. This indeed happened, but to a lesser extent

* Stalin promised Roosevelt to go to war against Japan three months after the surrender of Germany. He kept his word to the day. His proclamation of war spoke of avenging Russia's defeat by Japan in 1905 (when Russia's humiliation and Japan's triumph had been welcomed by Lenin).

than he could expect. Rumania and Slovakia, his satellites, declared war on Russia instantly, as did Mussolini's Italy and Finland, Hungary a few days later,* and Franco sent an entire volunteer division to fight on the German side. Yet while the idea of a German-led crusade against Communism threw off some sparks, it was nothing like a wildfire. A prime example of selective inclinations is the, later famous, sermon of the Catholic archbishop (later cardinal) of Münster, Count Clemens von Galen, who in early August 1941 publicly declared anathema the National Socialist practice of killing the maimed and the insane — but in that same sermon Galen praised the decision of the Führer to invade Russia and fight a crusade against atheistic Communism. (Hitler understood this: he ordered that no measures be taken against von Galen for the time being; indeed, that crucifixes be restored in schoolrooms in Bavaria, where an overeager gauleiter had ordered them removed).

Perhaps the most horrible of the consequences of 22 June 1941 involved the mass murder of Jews living in Europe and in the provinces of the Soviet Union overrun by the Germans. The government of the Third Reich had arranged and executed many dreadful and, on occasion, murderous

---

* The pretext of the Hungarian government was that Russian bombs had fallen on Kassa, a city in Hungary, on 26 June. More than sixty years later this issue is still disputed. Fragments of evidence fortify my opinion that this incident had been clandestinely mounted by the German Abwehr, in collusion with some Hungarian officers.

measures against Jews both in Germany and beyond before June 1941; but before that the main policy of the Hitlerian regime was the expulsion (or segregation), not — yet — the extermination of Jews. There exists no single document, no written or even oral instruction by Hitler, calling for a change of this policy, for the physical extermination of Jews; but most serious researchers indicate that such a change occurred latest by September 1941 — that is, soon after the German invasion of the Soviet Union. For then the largest aggregate of a Jewish population in the entire world, the millions of Jews in eastern Poland, the Ukraine, White Russia, Lithuania, Latvia, Bessarabia, Bukovina, fell under the sway of German rule. To the National Socialist mind they were, by their very nature, enemies of the Third Reich, whether potential or actual ones. They had to be liquidated, together with other Jews remnant in Germany or across Europe. Indeed, the first ordered and executed murders of masses of Jews occurred in July and August 1941, well before the later-infamous Wannsee Conference in January 1942 that decreed and arranged the deportation and extermination of Jews all over Europe and the western Soviet Union.

It is perhaps noteworthy that this high-level conference was first convoked for 8 December 1941 (the day after Pearl Harbor) and then postponed six weeks. Before that, the threatened and humiliated Jewish people across Europe and Russia breathed sighs of relief at the news, first, of Russia coming into the war on 22 June, and then of America's entering the war in December. That these two, to them starry, events would then be followed by their and their relatives' Holocaust was a consequence that they did not and could not know or even imagine.

3

We must now shift our attention from what may have been unintended to what was unexpected — on 22 June and for some time after that. That was the fighting capacity of the Russians. Their armies went from defeat to defeat, but they did not collapse. Stalin did not collapse either; but he had many days and nights of black despair. At times he tried to grasp the strangest of straws. On 3 September he sent a message to Churchill. The Soviet Union was "in mortal peril." The British ought to invade France or the Balkans and send to Russia "a minimum monthly aid of 400 aeroplanes and 500 tanks." Ten days later he asked Churchill to send twenty-five or thirty British divisions (through Archangel or Persia) to fight alongside the Russians. Churchill told him that this was impossible. He did not have the extra ships or the extra men. All that he could promise were more British arms shipments, more British bombing of Germany, and perhaps a British landing in northern Norway. He had to consider that a Russian surrender to Hitler was at least a possibility. But during that bleak and dark autumn of 1941, that danger was slowly, sometimes imperceptibly passing; and then, at the end of the first week in December, came a great change, almost at the same moment, in the Pacific and before Moscow.

And now the relations of the great warring powers, almost instantly, changed. After that unexpected military turning point of the war loomed its unintended consequences. Soon Stalin would depend less on Britain and America than they would depend on him. Churchill saw that rather clearly. He knew what kind of people Stalin and his Russians were; but he also knew that without them the Western Allies could not conquer Hitler's Germany and win the world war.* The fear that Stalin might yet make a deal with Hitler haunted him until late into the war. It explains many of the unhappy compromises and concessions he made to Stalin throughout the war; it also explains his extreme wording of his phrases praising Stalin on occasion. (They were neither calculating nor entirely insincere; he came around to see in Stalin a statesman and a great war leader.)

---

* One striking example from Churchill's own words. In March 1942 he spoke with General Władysław Sikorski, head of the free Polish government in London. He admitted that "his own assessment of Russia did not differ much" from that of Sikorski; but "he underlined the reasons which made it necessary to conclude an agreement with Russia. She was the only country that fought against the Germans with success. She has destroyed millions of German soldiers and at present the aim of the war seemed not so much victory, as the death or survival of our allied nations. Should Russia come to an agreement with the Reich, all would be lost. It must not happen. If Russia was victorious she would decide on her frontiers without consulting Great Britain; should she lose the war, the agreement would lose all its importance." *Documents of Polish-Soviet Relations, 1939–1945* (London, 1961), 1:267–268.

But we are moving beyond the framework of this book, whose main figures are Hitler and Stalin. Yes, German rule over eastern Europe, including the conquest of at least portions of European Russia, was what Hitler always wanted. And yet his principal opponent was not Stalin but Churchill, before June 1941 as well as after, at least for a while. We have seen his argument before 22 June, that "when Russia is defeated, this will force England to make peace." And he continued with this argument after 22 June as well. He said to Field Marshal Wilhelm Keitel on 18 August: "The ultimate objective of the Reich is the defeat of Great Britain." On 22 August to General Franz Halder, who put it down in his war diary: Hitler's aim is "to finally eliminate Russia as England's allied power on the continent and thereby deprive England of any hope of a change in her fortunes." To Admiral Kurt Fricke on 28 October: "The fall of Moscow might even force England to make peace at once."* We must not discount the possibility that in speaking thus to his military leaders, Hitler's purpose was to impress them with his reasons for having gone to war with Russia, since at least some of them may have had doubts about a two-front war. Yet it was not only to his military auditors that he spoke thus; and, as I wrote earlier, his motives and purposes were compound and not simple.†

* Cf. Lukacs, *Hitler of History,* 149–152.

† See above, pages 12, 26, 91. The excellent German military historian Gerd B. Ueberschär and his coauthor, Lev Bezymensky, properly argue (*Der deutsche Angriff,* 13): "The 'Festlandsdegen-Motiv' [the idea of Rus-

Even before Moscow and Pearl Harbor there is a stunning piece of evidence of Hitler's powers of foresight; or, in other terms, of a change in his mind. On 19 November he dropped this remark to General Halder in his headquarters: "The recognition, by both of the opposing coalitions, that they cannot annihilate each other leads to a negotiated peace." Four days later Halder recorded another of Hitler's remarks in his war diary: "We must face the possibility that neither of the principal opponents [Germany and Britain] succeed in annihilating, or decisively defeating, the other."* Note that Hitler spoke thus when on the central front Fedor von Bock's army was still inching forward to Moscow, more than two weeks before Zhukov began to push the Germans back before Moscow, and more than two weeks before Pearl Harbor brought the United States into the war. More important: now his entire war strategy changed. He knew that he could no longer win *his* war, his war of short wars. But he also knew that he had not — yet — lost it; that he could force one or another of his enemies to negotiate an armistice or peace with him. His model was no longer a super-Bismarck; it was now Frederick the Great, who in the Seven Years' War, 1757–1763, won against an overwhelming but temporary coalition of his enemies by defeating (or eliminating) one of them, whereafter that coalition collapsed. Hitler believed

---

sia's being the last weapon for England in Europe] was not the decisive basis for Hitler's decision to go to war against the Soviet Union." Yes and no; or, rather, no; true, but not true enough.

* Halder, *Kriegstagebuch,* 3:295, 306.

that the unnatural coalition between Churchill and Roosevelt and Stalin, between capitalists and Communists, would not last; it would break up sooner or later. (And break up it did, but too late for him.) He also ordered the reformation of the German economy from a partial to a total wartime basis. He now prepared for a long war.* Ideologue and statesman: there are multiple evidences for that compound — as well as for the dualities in his mind.

So were there dualities within Stalin. We have seen that even before 1941 he thought of himself as statesman above all. We have also seen that his unwavering belief in the validity of his statesmanship led to the catastrophe on 22 June, with all of its consequences; yet he did not cease thinking of himself as a statesman and acting accordingly throughout the war. Litvinov once remaked that "Stalin does not know the West." Yes and no. He would, on occasion, regard Churchill and even Roosevelt as his clever adversaries. Yet cunning and suspicious as he was, he came around to trust Churchill and Roosevelt at least in one decisive matter: when Molotov or someone else once suggested that the Germans might lure the Anglo-Americans into a separate armistice, Stalin said that Churchill and Roosevelt would not do that. Now, finally, he preferred them to be his allies, not Hitler.

Yet a last few words may be in order to describe how Stalin and Hitler felt, thought, and spoke about each other

---

* And, unlike Napoleon's, his armies survived the Russian winter and their first forced retreats. Hitler in April 1942: "We have mastered a destiny which broke another man 130 years ago."

even after 22 June and during the war. More than one book has been written comparing the two; but regrettably including little or nothing about their relationship.* Stalin's respect for Hitler may be found in a few of his private remarks during the war. His daughter Svetlana remembered her father saying after it: "Together with the Germans we would have been invincible." On the other side there is ample evidence of Hitler's respect for Stalin. On one occasion he said that Stalin could be the only possible leader of a Russia, on another that if Stalin were to be captured, Hitler would set him up in a villa in Potsdam. More important: notwithstanding his public speeches, Hitler long before 1945 ceased to believe in "Jewish Bolshevism." He would scream about Jewish Bolshevism till the very end (as in his last public directive on 16 April 1945), but that was not at all what he thought. Among other matters he knew that Stalin, too, was anti-Semitic. (To this we may add another dreadful consideration: that neither Hitler nor Stalin showed much, if any, interest in the physical extermination of millions of Jews during the war.)

We have come to the end of our story. The wartime admiration of Stalin and Russia is another chapter of history. It would not last. In 1941 Russia seemed as yet another weak

---

*Alan Bullock's *Hitler and Stalin: Parallel Lives* (1992) is useless: a double chronological portrait, going back and forth, with almost nothing about their relationships, how Hitler and Stalin saw (and spoke) about each other.

and disorganized prey of the Third Reich. In 1945 Stalin's Russia was the greatest power in Eurasia, one of the two rulers of the entire globe, the only equal of the United States. That, too, would not last — again, mostly because of Stalin's character. In 1941 he failed because of his excessive trust in Hitler; after 1945 he failed because of his excessive suspicions of the United States. To explain this would call for another book. Here it may be enough to state that in 1945 and thereafter he feared American (and Western) friendship even more than American hostility. Had he accepted the American idea that the eastern part of Europe occupied by his armies would be governed by governments dependent on and respectful of Russia but not Communized and cut away from the rest of Europe,* there would have been no cold war, and Russia could have entered a new phase of its tragic history, rebuilt after the war, assisted and helped by American sympathies and funds. This did not happen. Stalin's view was that something like a Marshall Plan for eastern Europe and Russia would be yet another instrument to spread American influence within and into his sphere, reducing his influence and power. But then hardly more than forty years after 1945 (and less than three dozen years after his death), the Russian empire in eastern Europe collapsed, together with the Communist regime of the Soviet Union. So now America became the

---

* As happened to Finland, a unique case, principally because of Stalin's respect for the Finns.

only superpower in the world — one of the unintended consequences of Hitler's invasion of Russia in June 1941.

4

It is an unfortunately still current misconception of history that the historian, employing proper methods of his craft, can establish such a precise reconstruction of past events and their actors, nailing down such a record of a portion or section of history, that it thereafter remains definite, unchanging, and perennial. This is not so. It is not only that, unlike law, history allows its students to engage in multiple jeopardy — that is, to rethink and judge anew the records and the meaning of events and of their actors again and again. It is that the most important (and yes, perennial) duty of the historian is to struggle against the prevalence of untruths, since the pursuit of truth is often a struggle through a jungle of sentiments and twisted statements of "facts." Such misconceptions and misstatements include the tendency to regard most, if not the entire history, of the twentieth century as the combat between capitalism and Communism, or between "freedom" and "evil." Arguments about both Hitler's Preventive War and the Two-War Theory are consequent to that tendency. We must not underestimate the attraction of such ideological simplifications of history. Only a few years after the end of the Second World War it led in the United States to a revolution of sentiments, whereby anti-Communism became a powerful substitute (and often a veritable replacement) for American patriotism. Thirty years later it led to the triumphalist presidency of Ronald Reagan, who, thirty years after Stalin's death, kept naming the Soviet Union the Evil Empire, and arming the United States against it on land, on sea, in air, and in space. A few years later, when Communist rule began to collapse in eastern Europe, Reagan himself thought it best to revise some of his views. Yet as late as in October 1989, William F. Buckley, Jr., an influential public writer who had much to do with the "conservative" movement propelling Reagan to power, wrote in his magazine: "Would things have been better if Hitler had conquered Moscow? They could hardly have been worse." They would have been worse, because Hitler then would have become well nigh unconquerable — not forever, but for a painfully long time.

Of the two abovementioned but still prevalent misconceptions, the one about the Preventive War is easier to demolish. We have seen how nearly everything we know of Stalin's beliefs and words and acts before 22 June 1941 are proofs to the contrary of that. Add to this the evidence of German military documents at that time, according to which most, indeed all, Russian military preparations were "defensive." Consider, too, what Goebbels and his propaganda told the German people on 22 June: that the German war against Russia was to prevent Russia attacking. Hitler himself told Ribbentrop on 18 June: "Emphasize frontier incidents" in order to prove that his invasion of the Soviet Union was a preventive one. Yet this is what more than a half-century later some still believe (and write). The tendency to assert that Hitler merely anticipated Stalin's plan to attack him remains current, perhaps especially in Germany.*

Yet at least in most cases, the purpose of the Preventive War theorists is not to apologize for Hitler. It is, rather, to exonerate Germany's record in the Second World War. The still widespread inclinations and arguments of the Two-War Theory suggest that the Third Reich fought two wars, one against the West and another against Soviet Russia, of which the first was avoidable and regrettable, while the second was not; and that it was the shortsightedness of the West, and of Churchill and Roosevelt, not to recognize that. Beneath that lies the subtle, and sometimes not at all subtle, suggestion that Communism was as bad as National Socialism (yes, true for some people but not for others); and that National Socialism was but a reaction to the evils of Communism (which is largely untrue).

But then the subjects of this book are not Isms (or Wasms, as the English wag said in August 1939) but Hitler and Stalin. At least two generations separate us now from these two men. We may now see Hitler and Stalin as men of a transitional century. More: their lives were part of the end of an era that lasted, by and large, from 1500 to 2000, the — so-

---

* One example: General Heinz Trottner (retired General-Inspector of the democratic West German army) in 1997: what happened in June 1941 was "before everything, a Preventive War compelled and begun with a heavy heart." (Hitler's "heavy heart"!)

called — Modern Age. Different as that was for Germany and for Russia, they represented their reactions against — again the so-called — Enlightenment, or call it the Age of Reason; more accurately: against the world of a bourgeois civilization that reached its peaks around the time when they were born. What they were, and what they did, was and remains amazing. They were protagonists and leaders of their peoples: and yet, somewhat like Pyrrhus near the end of the great Hellenic age, captives of a past, of their own past, no matter how drastically they tried to transform it. Hitler and Stalin were giants. But it seems that Providence will not allow giants to rule the world, or perhaps even most of the world. What may be the ultimate meaning of the strange fact that the greatest instrument of the retribution of Germany and of the end of Hitler was Stalin's Red Army? It is, as a great Portuguese proverb says: God Writes Straight with Crooked Lines.

Appendix

The Mystery of Hitler's "Letter" and the Courier Plane

Hitler — allegedly — wrote two letters to Stalin during the six months before the twenty-second of June in 1941. These were — again, allegedly — responses to letters that Stalin had written to him. Two of Hitler's letters, one dated 31 December 1940, the other dated 14 May 1941, were printed in their entirety in David Murphy's recent book.* Of the two the later one may be of special interest.

I am reproducing its text:

* Murphy, *What Stalin Knew*, 256–258.

Appendix

May 14, 1941

Dear Mr. Stalin,

I am writing this letter at the moment of having finally concluded that it will be impossible to achieve a lasting peace in Europe, not for us, not for future generations, without the final shattering of England and her destruction as a state. As you well know, I long ago made the decision to carry out a series of military measures to achieve this goal.

The closer the hour of a decisive battle, however, the larger the number of problems I face. For the mass of the German people, no war is popular, especially not a war against England, because the German people consider the English a fraternal people and war between them a tragic event. I will not conceal that I have felt the same way and have several times offered England humane peace terms, taking into consideration England's military situation. However, insulting replies to my peace proposals and the continuing expansion by the English of the field of military operations with the obvious intention of drawing the entire world into war persuade me that there is no other way out of this situation except for an invasion of the Isles and the decisive destruction of that country.

English intelligence, however, has very cleverly begun to use the concept of "fraternal peoples" for its own purposes, applying it to its own propaganda, not without success.

Consequently, opposition to my decision to invade the Isles has drawn in many elements of German society, including individual members of the higher levels of state and military leadership. You are certainly aware that one of my deputies, Mr. Hess, in a fit of insanity, I suppose, flew to London, taking this unbelievable action, to the best of my knowledge, to awaken the English to common sense. Judging by information in my possession, similar moods have struck several generals of my army, particularly those who have distinguished relatives in England descending from the same ancient, noble roots.

In this connection, a special warning is raised by the following circumstance. In order to organize troops for the invasion away from the eyes of the English opponent, and in connection with the recent operations in the Balkans, a large number of my troops, about eighty divisions, are located on the borders of the Soviet Union. This possibly gave rise to the rumors now circulating of a likely military conflict between us.

I assure you, on my honor as a chief of state, that this is not the case.

From my side, I also react with understanding to the fact that you cannot completely ignore these rumors and have also deployed a sufficient number of your troops on the border.

In this situation I cannot completely exclude the possibility of an accidental outbreak of armed conflict, which given the conditions created by such a concentration of troops might take on very large dimensions, making it difficult if not impossible to determine what caused it in the first place.

I want to be absolutely candid with you.

I fear that some one of my generals might deliberately

embark on such a conflict in order to save England from its fate and spoil my plans.

It is a question of no more than a month.

By approximately June 15–20 I plan to begin a massive transfer of troops to the west from your borders.

In connection with this, I ask you, as persuasively as possible, not to give in to any provocations that might emanate from those of my generals who might have forgotten their duty. And, it goes without saying, try not to give them any cause. If it becomes impossible to avoid provocation by some of my generals, I ask you to show restraint, to not respond but to advise me immediately of what has happened through the channel known to you. Only in this way can we attain our mutual goals, on which, it seems to me, we are clearly in agreement.

I thank you for having agreed with me on the question known to you and I ask you to forgive me for the method I have chosen for delivering this letter to you as quickly as possible.

I continue to hope for our meeting in July.

Sincerely yours,

Adolf Hitler

Let me begin the analysis of this "document" with a personal note. My first reaction reading it was that this letter is a forgery—that is: not authentic, and not written by Hitler. My reason for this immediate impression was, and remains, that neither the contents nor the style of the letter is typical of Hitler. At the risk of presumption, allow me to add that this is the third occasion when I have been confronted with falsifications involving Hitler or his admirers: in both previous instances evidence proved that my initial doubts were correct.* However, let me now turn to the documentary evidence itself. There is no trace for such a correspondence (at least not now) in either the German or the Russian archives. It is of course possible that both Hitler (at the very end of his life) and Stalin destroyed such letters. But we have no evidence of such a decision from any one of their respective staffs, especially none on the German side. (After all, someone must have translated Stalin's letter into German, and someone else must have typed it for Hitler on his special large-lettered typewriter.) When, forty years after 1941, Molotov was asked about such letters, he said: nonsense. There is one, again alleged, evidence of their existence on the Russian side. In 1966 Marshal Zhukov was supposed to have had a conversation with two Russian writers, Konstantin Simonov, a journalist, and Lev Bezhimensky, a former diplomat and journalist. They include an episode when, on 15 June 1941, Stalin actually pulled out Hitler's letter from his desk

---

*The first instance, in 1981, was the appearance of the forged Hitler "diaries" (which, alas, serious historians at first accepted as real). I had not seen the "diary" but, knowing something about Hitler, I immediately thought that they were implausible, in part because of Hitler's disinclination to write (especially very late at night). The second instance, in 2001–2002, was the — very knowledgeable — falsification of a German transcript, allegedly read by Hitler, of an overheard and recorded telephone conversation between Churchill and Roosevelt in July 1943 — alas, printed in a book in the United States, with the obvious purpose to blacken Churchill. (See my article in *American Heritage*, November–December 2002.)

drawer and showed and read some of it to Zhukov. "Read it."* Yet, according to the erudite Russian historian Sergei Slutsch, Stalin never met Zhukov privately; according to the record of Stalin's appointments, certainly not on 15 June.

If we could see the actual document, analysis of the paper, of Hitler's signature, etc., could tell us something. What exist are transcripts. To this let me add that Hitler was usually very careful with his letters, in part because of his suspicion and dislike of the written word. A proof of that is his one truly authentic letter to Stalin on 20 August 1939, which is both indirect and very cautious, authorizing his Foreign Minister Ribbentrop to authorize in turn the German ambassador in Moscow to present himself to Molotov "and hand him the following telegram from the Führer to Herr Stalin." The text follows, after which: "Please deliver to Herr Molotov the above telegram of the Führer to Stalin in writing, on a sheet of paper without letterhead."†

But now we come to the origins of this alleged correspondence, the story of which may be significant enough not to dismiss this matter instantly. And this involves three meetings of two very different people, the two ambassadors: Schulenburg, the old aristocrat, a remnant incarnation of an

---

* Zhukov — again, allegedly: "I am afraid that after so many years I cannot exactly reproduce Hitler's words. But this I do remember precisely. . . . I read the TASS communiqué in the June 14 issue of *Pravda,* and in it, to my amazement, I discovered the same words I had read in Hitler's letter to Stalin in Stalin's office. That is, in this Soviet document, I found printed Hitler's arguments." Murphy, *What Stalin Knew,* 186–187.

† *NSR,* 66–67.

Old Europe, yet still employed in the foreign service of the Third Reich, and Dekanozov, a former subordinate of Beria, largely ignorant of Europe, uneducated and uncultured, a stump of a man. The initiative of their meeting came from Schulenburg, who was deeply depressed but also impressed by two things. One was how Hitler had received him but a week before, not listening much to his argument about Stalin's unwillingness to challenge Germany in any way. The other matter was Schulenburg's estimate of the, to him, immense importance of Stalin's assumption of the headship of the Soviet Union's government on 5 May.* Schulenburg now asked Dekanozov to come (for breakfast) to the German embassy. Dekanozov was in Moscow. (On 1 May, Stalin made Dekanozov stand next to him at the customary grand parade on Red Square, suggesting to the world — and of course to Berlin — how important his relationship with Germany was.) Dekanozov did not know German. His interpreter Pavlov and Schulenburg's counselor Hilger were present. Schulenburg began the conversation: he said that something must be done to set Russian-German relations right. Dekanozov was at first wooden and cautious, saying little or nothing. Schulenburg said that they must discuss this matter further, that they should meet again before Dekanozov returned to Berlin. Four days later, on the 9th, Dekanozov asked Schulenburg to meet in the guest house of the

---

* It is not certain how Schulenburg knew of the Politburo's decision to elevate Stalin to that post, taken late the previous evening, though not officially announced until the 6th.

Soviet Foreign Ministry. (Probably their talk was tapped there.) There is every reason to believe that between 5 and 9 May, Dekanozov had met with Stalin and Molotov. This time the conversation of the two ambassadors went on for two hours. Schulenburg talked in an open, even daring, manner. He said that Hitler was "dissatisfied" with Russia. Dekanozov said that a possible move could be a declaration, or communiqué, issued jointly by Moscow and Berlin, asserting the peaceful intentions of the two powers. Schulenburg said yes, but there was a need to speed things up. It would be best if Stalin were to write such a letter to Hitler, who then could send his answer through a courier on a special airplane, so that the matter could be settled promptly.*
The next day (10 May) Stalin and Molotov ordered the expulsion of the Belgian and Norwegian and Greek and Dutch and Yugoslav legations from Moscow. On 12 May, Schulenburg and Dekanozov met again, in the German ambassador's residence. Surely there was need to hurry: Dekanozov was returning to Berlin by train that late afternoon. Now he was less cautious than Schulenburg. According to his summary: "I now took the initiative." Schulenburg began their conversation: a diplomatic courier had arrived with nothing new from Berlin. Dekanozov said that he had talked with Stalin and Molotov.† (He actually had Molotov's writ-

* *1941 g,* doc. 454.
† They certainly knew of Schulenburg's inclinations and intentions. Among other things, the Soviets wired the Moscow apartment of General Ernst von Köstring, the Germany military attaché; they overheard Schu-

ten instructions.) They told him that they agreed in principle about an exchange of letters; that the joint communiqué should refer only to Russia and Germany; that Stalin had said that Schulenburg should discuss the contents of a letter and of the possible communiqué with Molotov. Schulenburg said that he had no authority for that. He repeated that it would be best if Stalin were to send a personal message to Hitler; but he had to emphasize to Dekanozov "not to reveal him as the originator of this proposition"; perhaps sometime in the future he might mention it in his memoirs.[*]

Did Stalin write such a letter to Hitler? Not only is there no evidence for that anywhere; more significantly, nothing of that was mentioned either by Dekanozov or by his son Reginald.[†] If such a letter existed it would have been

---

lenburg talking to the latter, rather bitterly and desperately, about the failure of his intentions to avert war with Russia. On one occasion Schulenburg said that his efforts with Hitler had been fruitless; if he were to insist much more he might even end up in one of Himmler's concentration camps . . .

Count Friedrich Werner von der Schulenburg, allegedly marked by the anti-Hitler conspirators to become the foreign minister of a future Germany, was executed on Himmler's orders in November 1944. Neither he nor his family left memoirs.

[*] *1941 g*, docs. 458, 462. Once more — unnecessarily — Dekanozov asked Schulenburg whether their conversation had been proposed by the German government. Of this conversation neither Schulenburg nor his counselor Hilger left notes. Schulenburg insisted that he was talking to Dekanozov privately.

[†] A short typewritten summary of German-Russian relations by the latter was given to Montefiore. Dekanozov, close to Beria, was executed on the orders of Khrushchev and Co. in 1953.

carried to Berlin by Dekanozov himself, arriving in Berlin on the 13th. We saw that Hitler's "answer" to Stalin is dated 14 May—if so, in somewhat unusual haste. Yet there are at least two matters in that—I repeat, alleged—Hitler letter that call for some consideration; that, in plain English, make one think. One of them is Hitler's last sentence: "I ask you to forgive me for the method I have chosen for delivering this letter to you as quickly as possible"—a reference to a mysterious courier plane. There is some—though very little— evidence that on 15 May a German airplane flew to Moscow, "through Soviet airspace, undetected and apparently unauthorized and, against all regulations, landed at the central [Moscow] airfield. Here it was not only allowed to land but also refueled for its return trip and permitted to leave Soviet airspace."* There is but one Russian article about this implausible and nearly incredible event. Hitler had his favorite and confidential pilots, in whose memoirs there is nothing about this. And: what happened to the Hitler letter after the pilot landed in Moscow? It must have been delivered by someone somewhere, translated, taken to the Kremlin, etc., etc. (And why not through the German embassy, where Hitler knew what Schulenburg's inclinations were?)

The other matter—so implausible as to be nearly senseless—is Hitler's repeated statement about his potentially disobedient and reactionary and pro-British generals, attacking

---

* Murphy, *What Stalin Knew*, 190 et seq., about the fate of those Russian air force officials who were—again, allegedly—implicated in that event.

Russia against his instructions "in order to save England from its fate and spoil my plans."* Anyone who knows anything of Hitler and of the Third Reich and of its generals would say then, as indeed now: if you are ready to believe this, you are ready to believe anything. And Stalin did. But still, the question remains: why? We have seen that he trusted Hitler to the very end; indeed, he respected him even beyond that. As Pascal once said, love is not blind. It is, rather, that the lover's eye focuses differently, when a wish is the father of a thought. Stalin's principal conviction was that Hitler would not start a two-front war while still fighting with England. But, latest by early June, the mass of evidence that Germany might attack him had become so large and so overwhelming that it is not reasonable to think that his mind simply refused to look ahead. What now happened was a small but significant twist in his vexed mind: the idea that Hitler was one thing and the German military another, that Hitler would not attack him but that some of his generals might. But was this inclination a result of Hitler's letter? Or—was it fortified by Hitler's letter? I do not think so. I think that there was no such letter; I do not even think that it may have been confected on Hitler's orders. Was it forged on Stalin's orders? That, too, is unlikely. Perhaps—perhaps— it was confected by someone posthumously, for the purpose

---

* Yet another oddity: Hitler's phrase, very unusual for him: "I assure you, on my honor as a chief of state . . . " echoing Stalin's unexpected words in August 1939: "The Soviet government . . . gives its word of honor that the Soviet Union will never betray its partner."

of whitening Stalin's record, his responsibility for his self-imposed blindness in June 1941. (Note that in Hitler's letter there is no reference to or acknowledgment of a letter from Stalin.) Yes, Hitler knew what Stalin wished to believe, letter or not. But whatever happened during those ten days, 5 to 15 May 1941, whether they wrote to each other or not, did not change the final course of events.

Documents, Books, and Articles Consulted

As I conclude this book, there may be close to one thousand books and articles dealing with the year 1941 published in Russia during the past fifteen years. Some of these are more available than are others; some of them employ documents of questionable authenticity; in any event, they must be read in Russian. This alone makes their listing for the purpose of a more or less exhaustive (or even precise) bibliography in English necessarily incomplete. The governmental archives wherefrom some of the authors took their materials — the Archive of the Presidency of the Russian Federation (former archive of the Politburo and Archives of the Foreign Commissariat), the Russian State archives, the Russian State War Archives — were, and remain, only partially open for researchers, and access to them varies by occasion. To this I must add the general warning that history does not wholly consist of documents, while at the same time documents consist of history: who wrote them, and when, and why, and for whom, and for what purpose? — considerations especially unavoidable when it comes to papers written by and for officials in a police state.

The most important and most reliable documentary collection, including more than 650 documents leading up to 22 June 1941, is *1941 g.,* my abbreviation of *1941 god,* vol. 2 (March–June 1941), collected, annotated, and published by a group of scholars under the presidency of A. N. Yakovlev, Moscow, 1998. I have read many of these documents as they were translated for me.* What follows is a list of those other documents, books, and articles that I consulted during the writing of this book. This list is in alphabetical order, without comment on the contents or of the particular value of sources.

Actes et documents du Saint-Siège relatifs à la Seconde Guerre mondiale. Vol. 1. Vatican City, 1965.

Akten zur deutschen auswärtigen Politik, 1918–1945. Serie D, vols. 10–11.

Barros, James, and Richard Gregor. *Double Deception: Stalin, Hitler, and the Invasion of Russia.* DeKalb, Ill., 1997.

Below, Nicolaus von. *Als Hitlers Adjutant, 1937–1945.* Mainz, 1980.

---

* Especially nos. 437, 439, 454, 461, 462, 473, 493, 494, 512, 520, 522, 543, 552, 560, 561, 562, 574, 577, 581, 608, 611, 613, 651.

Belozerov, A. P. *Sekrety Gitlera na stole u Stalina.* Moscow, 1995.

Besymenski, Lew. *Stalin und Hitler: Das Pokerspiel der Diktatoren.* Berlin, 2002.

Bonwetsch, Bernd. "Stalins Äusserungen zur Politik gegenüber Deutschland, 1939–1941." In Ueberschär and Bezymenskij, *Der deutsche Angriff,* 145–164.

——. "Was wollte Stalin am 22. Juni 1941?" *Blätter fur deutsche und internationale Politik,* 1989, Heft 6.

Bunich, Igor. Operatsiia *"Groza."* Moscow, 1997.

Chizikov, N. Article in *Komsomolskaya Pravda,* 24 February 2002.

Chuev, Feliks. *Molotov Remembers: Inside Kremlin Politics,* ed. Albert Resis. Chicago, 1991.

Churchill, Winston S. *The Gathering Storm.* Boston, 1948.

——. *The Grand Alliance.* Boston, 1950.

Colville, J. *The Fringes of Power: Downing Street Diaries, 1939–1955.* New York, 1985.

Dimitrov, Georgi. *The Diary of Georgi Dimitrov,* ed. Ivo Banac. New Haven, 2003.

Elvin, Harold. *A Cockney in Moscow.* London, 1958.

Erickson, John. *The Road to Stalingrad: Stalin's War with Germany.* New Haven, 1999.

Fleischhauer, Ingeborg. *Die Chance des Sonderfriedens: Deutsch-sowjetische Geheimgespräche, 1941–1945.* Berlin, 1986.

Gillessen, Günther. "Der Krieg der Diktatoren." *Frankfurter Allgemeine,* 29 August 1988.

Glantz, David M., ed. *The Initial Period of War on the Eastern Front, 22 June–August 1941.* London, 1993.

Goebbels, Joseph. *Die Tagebücher von Joseph Goebbels: Sämtliche Fragmente.* Vol. 4. Munich, 1987.

Gorodetsky, Gabriel. *Grand Delusion: Stalin and the German Invasion of Russia.* New Haven, 1999.

Halder, Franz. *Kriegstagebuch: Tägliche Aufzeichnungen des Chefs des Generalstabes des Heeres, 1939–1942,* vol. 3, *Der Russlandfeldzug bis zum Marsch auf Stalingrad (22.6. 1941–24. 9. 1942),* ed. H.-A. Jacobson. Stuttgart, 1964.

Hilger, Gustav, and Alfred G. Mayer. *The Incompatible Allies: A Memoir-History of German-Soviet Relations, 1918–1941.* New York, 1971.

Kynin, G. P. "Unbekannte Aufzeichnungen von weiteren Unterredungen Schulenburgs mit Dekanosov in Mai 1941." *Berliner Jahrbuch für osteuropäische Geschichte,* 1994, vol. 1.

Lukacs, John. *The Duel.* New York, 1991.

———. *The Hitler of History.* New York, 1998.

———. *The Last European War, 1939–1941.* New York, 1976.

Messerschmitt, Manfred. In Pietrow-Ennker, *Präventivkrieg?*

Montefiore, Simon Sebag. *Stalin: The Court of the Red Tsar.* New York, 2004.

Murphy, David E. *What Stalin Knew: The Enigma of Barbarossa.* New Haven, 2005.

Nabojshchikov, G. Article in "Nevski Vremya," 22 February 2004.

Nazi-Soviet Relations, 1939–1941. Documents from the archives of the German Foreign Office. Department of State, 1948.

Nekrich, A. M. *Pariahs, Partners, Predators: German-Soviet Relations, 1922–1941.* New York, 1997.

———. In *"22 June 1941": Soviet Historians and the German Invasion,* ed. Vladimir Petrov. Columbia, S.C., 1968.

Nevezhin, V. A. *Sindrom nastupatelnoy voiny: Sovetskaia propaganda v preddverii "sviashchennykh boev," 1939–1941.* Moscow, 1997.

———. "Stalin's 5th May Address: The Experience of Interpretation." *Slavic Military Studies* 2 (March 1999).

———. *Zastolnye rechi Stalina: Dokumenty i materialy.* Moscow, 2003.

Orwell, George. *The Collected Essays, Journalism, and Letters of George Orwell,* ed. Sonia Orwell and Ian Angus. Vol. 2. London, 1968.

Pavlov, L. G. Article in *Voenno-istorichesky Zhurnal,* no. 6, 1990.

Pietrow-Ennker, Bianka. "Deutschland im Juni 1941 — ein Opfer sowjetischer Aggression?" *Geschichte und Gesellschaft,* 1988.

———. ed., *Präventivkrieg? Der deutsche Angriff auf die Sowjetunion.* Frankfurt, 2000.

Pleshakov, Constantine. *Stalin's Folly: The Tragic First Ten Days of World War II on the Eastern Front.* Boston, 2005.

Roberts, Cynthia A. "Planning for War: The Red Army and the Catastrophe of 1941." *Europe-Asia Studies* 47 (1992), vol. 47, 8.

Rozanov, L. G. *Stalin-Hitler, 1939–41.* Moscow, 1991.

Schroeder, Christa. *Er war mein Chef: Aus dem Nachlass der Sekretärin von Adolf Hitler.* Munich, 1985.

Schustereit, Hartmut. *Vabanque: Hitlers Angriff auf die Sowjetunion, 1941.* Herford, 1988.

Slutsch, Sergey. "Stalins 'Kriegszenario 1939': Eine Rede die es nie gab." *Vierteljahrshefte für Zeigeschichte,* 2004 / 4.

———. "Stalin und Hitler 1941. Kalkül und Fehlkalkulationen der Kreml." Unpublished ms., forthcoming in *Vierteljahrshefte für Zeitgeschichte.*

Stegemann, Bernd. "Geschichte und Politik: Zur Diskussion uber den deutschen Angriff auf die Sowjetunion." *Beitrage zur Konfliktforshung,* 1987.

Sudoplatov, Pavel. *Special Tasks: The Memoirs of an Unwanted Witness, a Soviet Spymaster.* Boston, 1994.

Suvorov [Rezun], Viktor. *Icebreaker: Who Started the Second World War,* trans. Thomas B. Beattie. London, 1990.

Ueberschär, Gerd R., and Lev A. Bezymenskij, eds. *Der deutsche Angriff auf die Sowjetunion, 1941: die Kontroverse um die Präventivkriegsthese.* Darmstadt, 1998.

Vierteljahrshefte fur Zeitgeschichte. Munich.

Volkogonov, Dmitri. *Stalin: Triumph and Tragedy,* ed. and trans. Harold Shukman. London, 1991.

Voss, Stefan. *Stalins Kriegsvorbereitungen, 1941.* Hamburg, 1998.

Weber, Reinhold W. *Die Entstehung des Hitler-Stalin Paktes 1939.* Frankfurt, 1980.

Wette, Wolfram. "Über die Wiederbelebung des Antibolschewismus mit historischen Mitteln." In *Geschichtswende? Entsorgungsversuche zur deutschen Geschichte.* Freiburg, 1987.

Whaley, Barton. *Code Word Barbarossa.* Cambridge, Mass., 1974.

Zoller, Albert. *Hitler Privat.* Düsseldorf, 1949.

Index

Index

Murphy, D., 72n, 74n, 75n, 77n, 147, 152n, 156
Mussolini, B., 11, 17, 23, 25, 29n, 32, 37, 39, 41, 50, 58, 64, 92, 113, 133

Nadolny, R., 14
Napoleon I, 1, 2, 39, 90, 139n
Negrín, J., 106n
Nekrich, A. M., 51n, 72n
Nevezhin, V., 70n
Norway, 25, 62, 82, 109, 135

Ordzhonikidze, S., 48
Orwell, G., 102

Papen, F. von, 121
Pius XII, Pope, 112
Poland, 8n, 14, 16, 17, 18, 19, 20, 22, 23, 24, 40, 52, 54, 59, 60, 63, 68, 73, 76, 134
Poskrebyshev, A., 56n
Proskurov, I., 74

Raack, R. C., 70n
Raeder, F., 13n
Reagan, R., 143
Ribbentrop, J. von, 18, 19, 20, 23, 29, 30, 31, 36, 37, 52n, 54, 55, 56n, 59, 63, 65, 69, 83, 91, 96, 143, 152
Rommel, E., 39, 103
Roosevelt, F. D., 3, 21, 24n, 27n, 29, 35, 36, 73, 93, 103, 109,
110, 112, 118, 127, 130, 131, 132, 139, 144, 151n
Rumania, 26, 28, 29, 32, 34, 41, 62, 64, 76, 133
Rumanians, 80, 113

Scheliha, R., 75n
Schroeder, C., 93n, 119
Schulenburg, F. W. von der, 15, 28, 67, 68, 71, 83–84, 96, 121, 152–55
Schultze-Boysen, H., 75n
Shcherbakov, A. S., 99
Sikorski, W., 136n
Simonov, E., 151
Slutsch, S., 44n, 56n, 152
Slovakia, 133
Sorge, R., 74, 74n, 131
Speer, A., 21
Stalin, J. V.: his character, 44, 46, 51, 139; his dismissal of Litvinov, 19, 52–53; his drafts for Molotov, 65; his emphasis on "the state," 47–50; on 5 May, 68–69; his Germanophilia, 51–52; nationalism, his views on, 58–59; and the 1939 pact, 22–24; his opposition to war, 4; his "secret speech" (19 August 1939), 56; his promotion to prime minister, 68; and "spheres of interest," 60; on 10 March 1939, 51–52; his treaty with Yugoslavia, 34; on 12 April 1941, 66–67; his trust

.